What Millennials Really Want from Work and Life

What Millennials Really Want from Work and Life

Yuri Kruman

BUSINESS EXPERT PRESS

First published in 2019 by
Business Expert Press, LLC
222 East 46th Street, New York, NY 10017
www.businessexpertpress.com

ISBN-13: 978-1-94944-395-0 (paperback)
ISBN-13: 978-1-94944-396-7 (e-book)

Business Expert Press Human Resource Management and Organizational Behavior Collection

Collection ISSN: 1946-5637 (print)
Collection ISSN: 1946-5645 (electronic)

Cover and interior design by S4Carlisle Publishing Services Private Ltd., Chennai, India

First edition: 2019

10 9 8 7 6 5 4 3 2 1

Printed in the United States of America.

Dedication

I dedicate this volume to my wife, Jennifer Kruman, who has stood by my side through every challenge, massive and small, for almost a decade, with otherworldly patience. I love you more than you will ever know.

This is also for the tens of millions of too-patient, too-long-silent fellow millennials hustling and grinding out there to make something of themselves and improve the world in their own way, despite all the roadblocks in their way. Keep on keeping on, brothers and sisters. We'll get there before you know it.

This book owes a great deal to all the many naysayers, doubters, bad bosses, and sundry shmucks of all stripes and generations out there in all walks of life who have acted like the walking wounded and dead to me and so many others, projecting their trauma onto others. You have shaped my journey, steeled my resolve, made me more resourceful, and taught me to forgive (but never forget), despite everything. For that, accept my sincere thank you. There is hope for you, yet.

Lastly, this book would be impossible without my dear mother, Inna Kruman, plus an assortment of dear friends, especially Ilya Starobinets and David Alexander and many others, as well as rabbis, mentors, teachers, neighbors, listeners and readers, perfect strangers, and thousands of other people who have shown kindness without cause and have helped me in some way in my journey. You are legion and deeply appreciated.

Abstract

This book is perfect for leaders across the enterprise who have a difficult time attracting, retaining, understanding, communicating with, motivating, engaging, and otherwise developing their millennial employees and job candidates. Diving deep into millennial psychology and language using a potent blend of data and anecdotes, stories and history, *What Millennials Really Want from Work and Life* debunks the many myths around millennials pushed by sensationalist media, showing how millennials want many of the same things as other generations, just more quickly and in a different order and form.

Giving helpful context based on his own powerful and unlikely story of continuous struggle and overcoming massive challenges as a millennial, the author weaves a compelling narrative through the historical, psychological, linguistic, and other threads underlying the millennial experience at work and in life. Based on his in-depth analysis of data and trends, Kruman makes specific recommendations for corporate leaders looking to get—and keep and develop—top millennial talent into their ranks, diving deep into specific benefits, communication methods and tools, mission and vision, and other elements of branding relevant to millennial attraction, engagement, and retention. This book is likewise for early and mid-career millennials looking to better understand themselves and make compelling cases for improvements around the aforementioned in their own companies.

Keywords

millennial; millennials; workplace; work; mythology; business; self-help; data; multi-generational workplace; cross-generational; communication; benefits; strategy; retention; engagement; employee retention; employee engagement; turnover; employee turnover; Boomers; Gen X; Gen Z; psychology; language; habits; culture; workplace culture; employee experience; customer experience

Contents

Acknowledgments

This book is dedicated, first, to my wife, Jennifer, without whom this book would not have seen the light of day. This is also for the many bad and awful bosses and human resources (HR) people I've dealt with over the years, who have taught me just how important it is to put "human" before "resource," how *not* to treat employees if you want them to do their life's best work for you. While I have learned from many mentors' books, podcasts, and articles, nothing has taught me quite as much as my amazing consulting and coaching clients, who are too numerous to mention here. All together, all of the people referred to have propelled me down the path of HR transformation and employee experience consulting to fix HR for the tens of millions of millennials and others facing the same challenges I have.

Introduction

George Orwell said it best: "Every generation imagines itself to be more intelligent than the one that went before it, and wiser than the one that comes after it."

Millennials, the media's favorite whipping boy, are really in for it.

Aside from killing sitcoms, dating, marriage—plus sex itself—and more than just spending all our retirement funds on avocado toast, we're killing that most American of American institutions, the 9-to-5 work week.

Don't tell anyone, but we also caused global warming, killed Kennedy, and were traumatized by Hungry, Hungry Hippos. EVERY. LAST. ONE. OF. US.

Sorry, I didn't mean to yell. It's just that, being a millennial myself—admittedly an old millennial, an xennial even—I've heard and read a steady stream of millennial deprecation for years.

Before I actually researched the subject for my *Forbes* column and this book, I must admit I was myself complicit in making fun of my generation.

Entitled, flaky, selfie-obsessed, selfish, escapist, secular and cynical about religion, super liberal, obsessed with video games, disloyal, immature, not interested in marriage, glued to the smartphone and social media, unengaged at work, distrusting of institutions, too idealistic, and clueless about grave realities

But that wasn't *me*, right? As a respectably cynical ex-Soviet immigrant and family man with two kids having to pay bills and run a coaching/consulting business, surely, I was above all this pettiness. Wasn't I?

I was both wrong and right. It was true that being of the millennial generation delineated by two boomer academics didn't make me or any other millennial the complete embodiment of all alleged sins and/or virtues of the said generation.

But it was just as true that for all the high-brow, nostalgia-driven dosage of classical music, film, and literature and intellectual discussions in my youth, I was hardly uninfluenced by the technology, geopolitics and socioeconomic policy, content and media, language and psychology, or workplace trends of the times I lived in.

In short, I was equal parts DMX and Mozart, Facebook and Proust, chess and soccer, school debt rich and house poor, an observant Jew who enjoyed his art house cinema, a distrustful employee and an entrepreneur focused on empowering others, a Russian from Kentucky who married a French woman from Morocco, a fan of avocado toast who mostly made it at home, and most of all, a millennial finally at peace with being a walking contradiction.

Having a hyphenated, complex identity is hardly remarkable in our age, where globalism, gender fluidity, and constant reinvention are still glorified and embraced widely, but how common or prevalent is this aforementioned phenomenon for an entire generation in the United States, the West, and around the world? Is this a true inflection point or a historical flash in the pan like the Weimar Republic or early 1900s Paris?

The jury is still out on the front of history, but a detailed look at the available, present-day data about millennials' work and consumption habits, views on themselves and the state of the world, plus the timeline for milestone events like marriage and mortgage, can help us make sense of what is fact and what is myth.

Taken together with anecdotes, insights, and data from my work over the years with several hundred career and business coaching and consulting clients—the vast majority of them millennials—we will aim to demystify and determine with some clarity what exactly it is that millennials *actually* want from work and life.

To be crystal clear, this book is *not* about how millennials are *different* from previous generations. Whether or not we're wildly different or completely the same has little bearing on what we really, truly want from work and life.

Now let's dig in.

A Millennial Workplace Manifesto

(This is something I wrote up back in 2016 to express my manifold frustration with being an employee in four different industries and lots of different companies of all sizes.)

Hey (Boomer/Gen X) Future Boss,

I'm that annoying, selfish, selfie-taking, and entitled future employee you love to hate—the true millennial. Nowhere to run, you'll have to hire me—or someone like me—very soon. We're taking over, bro.

The trouble is, you've got me wrong. I'm not your enemy and not a parasite distraction—I'm your biggest asset.

Why's that, you ask. I'm pretty good at what I do. That and I know what others like me want to buy, consume, believe and then invest in, talk about and value in their lives.

Who am I, really, boss? I'm just a dude with a portfolio career who wants to make a difference in the world, do well, make a good name for you and for myself, get paid, get more responsibility, accomplish something, then get out. I've got big plans, you see. That doesn't make me selfish—just pragmatic.

What do I want from you and from your company? I'll tell you very frankly.

1. Provide **radical transparency**.

    Next time there is an all-hands meeting, tell me what the different teams are doing. Why are they doing it, with what success or failure? Tell me the company financials, product details, and the strategy. I'll handle it just fine—big boy.

    I want to hear about our marketing, our hiring and how the market looks. I want to know ahead of time what bonuses will look like and what I need to do to get a raise, a better title, people I will manage, and so on.

    When you show me (not just tell me) we're in a glass house, I'll think twice before throwing a stone.

2. Share **purpose and mission**.

    Why are we here? Why are we doing what we're doing, in the way we are? What are we working for all day and night? Why does my role here matter? What is the bigger purpose here? Tell me how we are saving lives or people's time or money—better if all three.

    This makes me feel like I'm doing something meaningful with a positive impact on people's lives.

3. Provide **quick, pointed feedback** on performance—both the bad and good.

If something's off, I want to know ASAP to course correct. Less formal and more regular is better.

There is nothing more that I appreciate than when you take your time (even a couple minutes twice a week) to motivate me and help me improve.

4. **Drop the micromanaging**.

Treat me like the capable professional you hired and just let me do my job.

5. **Be flexible with using more of my skills**.

I'm not just a one-hit Excel wonder or copywriting robot. Use me or lose me.

Toss me a bone—let me work on a side project with another team or another project where I know I can be instantly helpful.

It helps keep me motivated and feeling useful to the company— and will reliably improve your bottom line and make it more likely I'll stick around a while.

6. **Step up to the plate as a mentor.**

Or find me someone here who can help guide me in my career path.

This means meaningful one-on-one time outside of work—not just passing words exchanged at a team-building exercise or group lunch.

7. **Drop the unlimited vacation policy**.

In practice, this just means nobody ever takes off. Set an example by actually taking off time and encouraging us to do the same. It makes burnout less likely and helps us refocus, refresh, and come back ready to take on new challenges.

8. Flat hierarchy or not, **drop the corporate politics** and two-faced appeals to culture and values.

Lead by example with radical transparency (#1) and by treating people like adults (#22) and with consistent decency (#23).

9. **Make decisions quickly and transparently**.

Make everyone aware of how (and why) we're moving forward. That's how you get my buy-in, no matter whether we agree.

10. **Mix up the demographics**.

We need the gray hair and the tattoos, young grads and old fogies (seen *The Intern?*), women and men, people from different walks of life and backgrounds and industries, and everyone in between.

Don't let it get stale and boring with everyone looking and sounding the same. Everyone (the company first) benefits from a shared perspective and wisdom from all kinds of different people in the same space, working on the same problems.

11. **Give me time and resources for meaningful professional development.**

   Sponsor me for a General Assembly course, online course, or industry conference. I will forever be grateful for the exposure and experience. This is a big one.

12. **Give me 10 to 20 percent of my work time for side projects.**

   Don't just pay lip service to what Google does (or used to do well). Use this as a way to tap my creativity, and I'll find you new revenue streams, better, cheaper, faster ways to do things, build new products, and so on.

   Create an internal forum to gather and generate useful ideas from employees to help the company.

   Let me pitch you or whomever in management on my ideas and how I'd implement them. If you approve, let me run with them in balance with my existing tasks.

13. **Let me move around internally and outside of the company.**

   If I like what I learned from you, I'll work with you again in the future on the same or a new venture.

   Always be helpful to me in my career whether here or elsewhere and I'll always return the favor. No need to burn bridges just because I feel I should move on when I decide to.

14. **Drop the buzzwords and speak straight to me.**

   No more rocket ships, growth hacking, unicorns, Uber for whatever. No more synergies, efficiency, productivity, cost savings.

   I get that you drank the Kool-Aid, but don't make me drink it too. Speak plainly to me—or I'll think you're just another corporate tool or start-up douche.

   Oh, and drop that crappy Non-Disclosure Agreement (NDA). It's quite useless (unenforceable) and only breeds ill will.

15. **Give me benefits I'll actually benefit from.**

   Let me choose them myself, first of all. Offer benefits that fit my lifestyle and family situation. Show me that the company actually cares about my health and well-being, not just my productivity and its own bottom line.

For example, help me pay off my student loans, offer a 401(k) and/ or Roth Individual Retirement Account (IRA) match. Help me manage my finances by offering credit monitoring, identity theft protection, Health Savings Account (HSA) / Flexible Spending Account (FSA), other pretax investment opportunities.

Help me stay healthy by incentivizing earnings through walking 10,000 steps a day, not just with a cheaper gym membership. Start a pedometer competition with real rewards. Give me cash or good gift cards as inducement (Amazon, iTunes, etc.). The impact will be tremendous and long lasting—both for me and you.

16. **Don't nickel-and-dime me** on professional development, travel, and other things important for my job and overall performance.

17. **Stop offering gimmicks** (foosball table and endless snacks).

    We never have time to play foosball and just get fat from eating all day.

18. **Judge me on performance, not the hours I'm physically present in the office.**

    A weeklong, eight hours a day plus face time requirement in the office breeds hypocrisy and contempt, not to mention poor quality of work, absenteeism, and other evils. As long as I get the work done at a high level and remain motivated, much of the work I do can be done from almost anywhere.

19. **Be flexible with letting me work remotely.**

    I often do my best work at odd times. I likely have a kid, a wife, side projects, passions, volunteer activities. Sometimes it's best if I don't waste the time commuting in.

20. **Be consistently the same inside and out.**

    Don't be two-faced to me. I'll see right through it.

    Don't hire two-faced people who'll ruin your culture and drive the good people away. That's the number one ingredient that makes or breaks a company's success.

21. **Include me and other team members in candidate interviews.**

    This ensures that the whole group buys in before you hire someone who doesn't fit.

If I'm on the team, my opinion matters, so give me a voice on big decisions and hear me out. Don't just inform me of new team members the day they start or big changes after the fact. This is a BIG red flag.

22. **Treat me like an adult**—with dignity, respect and by giving me real responsibility and runway to accomplish my goals.

     Also, please respect my need for a life outside of work. Heard of *diminishing returns*? That is what happens when people work too many hours and start burning out.

     Give me an opportunity to do my best work with other smart and highly motivated folks on an important problem here that will have a real and positive impact on many people.

23. No need to be my best friend, but **be consistently decent to me and everyone else around**.

     Start a virtuous cycle of decency, and you'll reap the benefits many times over.

24. **Encourage everyone to recognize each other for a job well done**.

     Make them write it down for review time and factor it into compensation and bonuses. Motivation will go through the roof.

25. **Take hiring and HR very seriously**.

     Hire HR (and all other) people only when they *get it* and buy completely into the company's mission, purpose, and product.

     HR should be crystal clear about what motivates me and other employees, what each of us wants out of working here, and how to deliver it in return for my time, motivation, and best work. None of us should be treated like a commodity if you want us to stick around.

26. **Mix up the floor plan**.

     Don't force everyone to work out on the open floor all day with no room to breathe or hear our own thoughts. Leave room for people to work solo, so they can focus better.

     Now #KThanksBye.

                                    ***

CHAPTER 1

Debunking Myths about Millennials

Ever since millennials were old enough to enter the workforce in roughly 2004, and perhaps even earlier than that, bashing us has been big business for TV personalities, columnists, and the online commentariat.

Notable conservatives like Joe Scarborough, Senator Ben Sasse, and Rod Dreher have waxed condemnatory of millennials for perceived inability to communicate even with family members, addiction to video games, and laziness, immaturity, and social isolation.

The obsession with denigrating—or at least ignoring—millennials is actually a rare unifying cause for both sides of the isle, contributing to Hillary Clinton's lack of popularity among millennials despite their majority support for the Democrats in the 2016 election.

Among the most popular beliefs among the haters are that we are not politically active out of apathy and that we don't trust government and other institutions enough to attempt effecting change through them.

Talk of millennials destroying institutions through grassroots decentralization efforts, including blockchain for everything, may be jumping the gun, but not by much and not for long.

A lagging perception of economic and political dependence on boomer and Gen X bosses and elected representatives may be what's behind the outdated views.

The evidence, however, is strikingly to the contrary. While media reports right after the 2016 election spoke of millennial apathy, it turns out that a higher proportion of millennials (65 percent) voted in 2016 than the public at large (55 percent), according to a Vice Impact study.

In the almost 2 years since the 2016 election, millennial political activity has spiked dramatically in response to the Trump administration policies. And this is likely only the tip of the iceberg for what's coming, given the shocking primary win of Alexandria Ocasio-Cortez in New York, beating a 10-term incumbent.

Millennial spending power is also on the rise. Accenture projects millennial spending to increase by more than a factor of two from today to $1.4 trillion by 2020, representing as much as 30 percent of total projected retail sales.

It's clear that millennials are by and large no longer annoying, dependent teens, with most of us in our 20s and 30s already some years into our careers, many cohabiting or married and raising kids, owning homes and cars, and saving for retirement.

And in that vein, it turns out we're buying cars, after all. According to a 2018 study by the National Automobile Dealers Association, millennials are no different in terms of car ownership, with a higher automobile buying rate today than 10 years ago, even among the younger, single, and more urban subset. Only 19 percent of us would choose ridesharing over car ownership, according to the same study.

Oh, and we're also buying homes, despite the increasing prices and decreasing inventory. According to the real estate buying platform Trulia, the increase in those under 35 buying homes far outpaces the overall annual homeownership rate change. As long as the economy continues its strong run, this rate is likely to continue increasing.

Marriage and Religion

On the subject of marriage, it is indeed abundantly clear that millennials are marrying later than previous generations and marrying less, on average, at least to date, partly due to lack of economic security, but also because we are more likely to marry for romantic love and only after getting to know our romantic partner better. That said, millennials are no less likely to want to marry one day, with only 1 in 10 outright opposed to the institution of marriage, per se, which puts them on par with previous generations.

A larger proportion of millennials are cohabiting before or without marriage than previous generations, most even having children before or without getting married. Fewer are religiously observant, on average (more on this later).

As a whole, there has been an erosion of the effects of Judeo-Christian religious norms on—and the resulting stigmas around—marriage, birth control, cohabitation and rearing of children out of wedlock. In 2015, only 51 percent of Americans under 30 felt completely certain about the existence of G-d. Even so, millennials are just as spiritual, if not as religiously observant, on average.

On the side of social acceptance and legal protections, laws and regulations protecting married same-sex couples have been enacted in recent years. Just as importantly, benefits are now routinely extended by federal law and by corporate policy to domestic and same-sex partners. In short, you don't necessarily even need to get hitched to get health insurance or certain financial benefits.

Intermarriage with other religions and races is more likely than before in this generation. The attitudes around marriage and religion have undoubtedly become more liberal and protected by law, permitting true freedom to choose whom to marry, when, and if.

Habits

On the subject of bad habits related to smartphone and social media usage, the facts quickly deflate the premise that millennials are somehow *worse* or more addicted than Gen X or boomers. In fact, studies prove Gen Xers actually use social media more than millennials, on average. Smartphone usage for Gen X is nearly at parity with that of millennials, while tablet usage is even higher than for millennials. The pot is just as black as the kettle.

When we look at video game playing for millennials (18 to 34), as opposed to Gen X (35 to 54) and boomers (55+), we see higher rates of video game playing, although the effect size is tempered by the size of the millennial generation (75 million) and their age, which is prime for video game playing. That said, it bears noting that the average age for a gamer today is 35, 81 percent of children 13 to 17 play video games, and more than half of people from 30 to 49 (58 percent) play video games. Apparently, all age groups spend much time gaming, even those quick to point fingers at millennials.

As such, video game playing by millennials isn't a solely millennial vice or otherwise unexpected, given the age demographic, average *free time*, and upbringing, as compared with the generation immediately ahead (Gen X) and the generation behind (Gen Z).

When it comes to the on-demand economy for everything from cabs to dates, shares to likes, food to rooms, house help to toilet paper, experiences as much as goods, gaming, and media, with everything in between, millennials are often blamed for being impatient and demanding instant delivery, feedback, and overall, for demanding instant gratification.

But is this a millennial thing or just a structural behavioral shift for all consumers? After all, smartphone use and utilization of on-demand services are quite high for Gen Xers and growing quickly among boomers.

Interestingly enough, one study of customer experience actually suggests that millennials may be the most, rather the least, patient generation when it comes to waiting on the phone for customer service or not flipping out when the wrong drink or dish is served. Go figure.

While the jury is still out on how quickly the on-demand mindset will become the norm with the remaining boomers and Gen Xers with more traditional worldviews, the trends examined here suggest that impatience is very much a universal trait. With inevitably greater adoption of on-demand tools and mindset in all areas of life, it is perhaps unavoidable that we'll all be flipping out from noninstant delivery options before too long.

And the simple truth remains that time is the single most important nonrenewable resource for all humans, not just millennials.

Work

Finally, we take a magnifying lens to the workplace, that unholy grail of (alleged) millennial misdeeds, according to the cottage industry of corporate, academic, and political leaders bashing millennials.

To rehash, we've been called entitled, flaky, disloyal, unengaged, immature, unproductive (due to that social media obsession), distrusting of institutions, too idealistic, and clueless about the hard work it takes to move up in a corporate or political or academic hierarchy, and so on. Not to mention, we're killing the last remaining bastion of corporate control and respectability, the good old 9-to-5 work week.

Let's dive in to see what's fact and what's fiction here.

Let's look into average employee tenure, but first, a quick note about methodology.

In order to compare apples to apples, we must look at average tenure for Gen Xers and boomers at the same career stage, rather than compare the average tenure at one point in time, when older workers would obviously be more likely to stay in a job, being much more likely to have spouses, children, and mortgages, among other lifestyle cost commitments.

As such, when we look at average tenure for millennials at this stage in their careers versus Gen Xers at this stage in their careers, a *higher* percentage of millennials are actually staying 13 months or longer in their job than the Gen X cohort at a comparable time in their career. When we look at the percentage of millennials versus Gen Xers staying 5 years or more in their job at this stage, it is essentially the same percentage.

The narrative that young people tend to job-hop in a healthy economy has been around for a couple of generations before ours, and the data is squarely behind it.

If anything, *job churn*, a measure of job-hopping—and by implication, employee loyalty—has declined overall since 2000, with the average tenure for young people remaining flat since the 1980s, going from 2.9 years in 2006 to 2.8 years in 2016.

And this is the case despite the stagnant wage growth, disappearance of pensions and lack of meaningful wage insurance, watering down of health and financial benefits for employees and their families, plus weakened labor protections.

In fact, according to Rick Wartzman, author of *The End of Loyalty: The Rise and Fall of Good Jobs in America*, "good jobs" are those "that offer a decent wage, job security, good, 'defined' benefits, including affordable health insurance and a safe way of having money set aside for retirement." These "purple squirrel" jobs are increasingly difficult, if not impossible to find.

Beyond the job-hopper myth, one of the other most pernicious and damaging myths about millennials is that we're entitled and lazy and all about short-term perks, especially flexible work arrangements.

When we look at the actual data surrounding factors like productivity, loss of vacation days due to workaholism (also known as *vacation shame*) and work martyrdom, it quickly becomes clear that millennials are the highest proportion of those employees who work long hours, take the least average vacation days of any age cohort, and qualify as *work martyrs*.

Odd enough, the disparity between perception and reality. Experts explain this effect from three perspectives. One is the 24/7 connectedness millennials are used to, implying there is no real *disconnect* at the end of the work day. The other is the pernicious millennial anxiety about a weak economy and the fear of being fired or not being promoted, acquired in the Great Recession. Both perpetuate the always-present, always-connected habits of millennials in the workplace.

Lastly, we are likely seen as entitled and lazy precisely *because* we are more productive and tech savvy and need to feel a meaningful connection to the company mission. Based on how corporations and institutions have indeed failed us, their often arbitrary and hypocritical hierarchies and rules around promotions and raises make us question—openly, as opposed to in private—why things can't be done better in the here and now, not after the annual performance review.

Millennials are big on personal and professional development, a subject many (most?) corporations see as a waste of resources and time, since millennials tend not to stick around very long, in their mind (a self-fulfilling prophecy). Digital nativity and constant connectedness, coupled with Fear of Missing Out (FOMO), may also just breed boredom at work.

***

And so, the house of cards begins to crumble... The facts about us seem to tell a wildly different story from the one being pushed by gurus and the talking heads that scare and demonize millennials.

As the facts show, our Maslow's hierarchy of needs is the same as everyone else's, both in life overall and at work, if with certain generational differences that are real and meaningful. But for the things we want from life, whether it be material, spiritual, social, professional or otherwise, we're mostly like all the generations that came before us.

Our approach, ethos, level of patience, and life stage may be different from grumbling Gen Xers and boomers, but most of the differences are the same differences that show up for every generation maligned by the ones who parent and grandparent it. And in the workplace, these differences originate in the divergent mindsets and incentives of middle management versus "the kids" versus the C-suite.

It's hardly news that older people tend to be more conservative and set in their ways than younger people.

Despite all the bloviating about us in the media, we millennials are not purposely destroying anything, as much as we're adjusting to the reality we've been given in adulthood. The hand we were dealt with the Great Recession, outdated and often irrelevant college education, high prices of housing and education, high debt load, low social mobility, and a world full of uncertainty has been quite difficult for a great many of us.

We already know we're worse off than previous generations, not least because of the policies of our gerontocracy in Congress and the Oval Office.

Despite the many and great benefits we have in living in America in our slice of time, there are serious challenges that we must contend with if we are even to desire sustaining the illusion of a meritocracy or a democratic rule of law for everyone. You can't blame us Millennials for being cynical.

Maybe we are in many ways just as boring and conventional as the blowhards ahead of us in age, except we're less financially secure, more anxious about it, and have no effective power to reshape the laws and policies and hierarchies that scapegoat us, keep us indebted and compliant, and screw over us and our socioeconomic trajectory as a generation.

Or, more likely, we're just waiting for our moment of sunshine to step forward, which may not ever materialize.

Many of us are indeed still hurting from the impact of the Great Recession and from the structural problems of our economy. But most of us are long up and out of our proverbial parents' basement and making a life for ourselves.

Like it or not, agree or disagree, the kids are all right. (You know, sort of. #KiddingNotKidding.) Just as they always have been.

***

Summary

Debunking Myths about Millennials—we're not destroying all institutions and existing business models, but improving them quickly and getting rid of invalid ones; what is truth and what is fiction, establishing the facts on the ground about millennials and exposing *experts* who purport to know and speak for us.

NOTES

- Tenure is the same as for previous generations at this stage
- Flexible work arrangements are key
- Personal and professional development
- Want to be part of something greater than themselves, part of a strong mission
- Want to make an impact on the world
- Want to move up quickly, learn, take on more responsibility
- Loyalty is seen as a two-way street and not critical to career or professional or personal development
- Have a view of entrepreneurship as glamorous, lucrative, or prestigious versus the view of the previous generations and Gen Z

***

Further Reading

Richie Norton debunks a few more millennial myths

***

So, instead of blaming us for all earthly ills, learn from us and help us to make the world you left for us better.

***

Why have millennials not fought back at these characterizations, at least not systematically?

Much of it has to do with age, stage in life, and lack of power through politics, media and other channels.

- lack of transparency due to distrust of institutions and corporations (data leaks and scandals)
- precarious financial situation—being saddled with debt, being unable to secure meaningful full-time employment, dependence on a financial system stacked toward the rich and powerful (highly peopled by boomers and Gen Xers), plus relative lack of spending power, underrepresentation in boardrooms and halls of power, and so on
- essentially forced to play by the rules of others, which we had no hand in making, have little to no voice in changing laws and policies and no political or economic power to force large-scale changes in the financial services or political systems
- ruled by a gerontocracy that blames us for every earthly ill, even while taking little responsibility for leaving us a legacy of war, recession, underemployment, poor financial health and literacy, a broken political system, and an economy that skews heavily toward the already wealthy
- small and shrinking social mobility in the United States and other wealthy Western countries

**

Judging by the volume of digital ink spilt on blaming millennials for the death of everything that is good and holy, including matrimony, the news media and online commentariat primarily composed of Gen Xers and boomers have gone to town with blaming millennials for the death of nostalgia, itself.

**

CHAPTER 2

Personal History as Guide

Author's story and how it's uniquely emblematic of the millennial experience, trauma, dislocation, disruption, and decentralization

> *It's gonna get a lot worse, again and again and again, before it gets better. But you have everything you need in your life to get through all the massive setbacks and challenges, not just to survive, but to thrive.*

> *Just apply yourself, get over your hang-ups and fears, and take risks, but intelligently. Guard your time zealously, above everything else. Deal with problems head on by learning from those who have actually solved them successfully and applying their lessons.*

> *Never be afraid to ask "dumb" questions or to ask for help. Better to apologize than to ask permission. Never be the smartest guy in the room. Never be sorry for yourself. Know yourself and always work hard to become a better version of yourself.*

> *Be resourceful and learn from everyone, both for the good and the bad.*

If I could give my 21-year-old self any advice at college graduation, it would be the aforementioned words. Instead, I had some annoying guy named Bono (yep, that one) telling me to save Africa as he got his honorary . . . law degree.

No secret that hindsight is always 20/20 and the human mind tends to regret, romanticize, forget, or wrongly remember certain episodes, especially after the fact, in *greener pastures*.

With that in mind, I'll stick to the relevant parts of my life experience for our discussion of millennials at work and in life.

To preface my working life, it's worth noting the direction from which I came to it, even before the four career changes, several stretches of unemployment, a slew of bad bosses, and the rest.

The story starts in Moscow, where I was born in 1983, 36 days after the end of Season 3 of *The Americans*, which is to say after the day Reagan called the USSR an *evil empire* in a famous speech. Paige had just seen her grandma for the first and last time. On the exact day of my birth, April 13, the United States performed a nuclear test in Nevada.

Like most Soviet kids, I grew up in simple, Soviet circumstances in a small town of 20,000—an academic town full of scientific institutes where both of my parents worked—about 2 hours south of Moscow. Mom worked in the biophysics institute and dad worked in the microbiology institute.

Both had already been immigrants once, with mom leaving Kazakhstan at 10 for Moscow and father moving after college to Moscow for grad school from Kharkov. They'd met at Moscow State University and married quickly, not least so they could trade up for a better apartment, as was typical back then. After a year, my sister was born, later proving to be a stereotypically pessimistic first-born and cynical Gen Xer.

The four of us lived with grandma in a two-bedroom apartment with a dog. The house was always full of books, which my father enjoyed collecting.

When I was five, my parents divorced and dad started a new family right away. We moved into a larger apartment where my sister, who's always been a talented painter, painted the doors and hung up her model drawings.

My Soviet childhood was mostly happy in that we got to roam around freely, whether on the playground without padding or in the forest, catching May beetles, picking berries and mushrooms, and otherwise learning about life while parents were at work. Mom read a lot to me, especially about archaeology and languages, literature. We memorized poetry for class. I even played a king with a backless throne in the school play, although I distinctly recall freezing up and forgetting my lines. It was an auspicious start to a speaking career.

I read a lot after learning how at the age of 4, learned geography with a passion, tortured my fair share of insects with a magnifying glass, like any young boy. We visited mom's parents on the other side of Moscow, seeing her younger sister's and brother's families, helping grandparents keep their Eden-like orchard in shape, picking strawberries and raspberries, plums and cucumbers, squashes and apples, among others. It was an idyllic time.

The town we lived in was picturesque, and I have many wonderful memories of its bazaar and forests, the old, overgrown aristocratic mansion where a semifamous movie had once been shot. Divorce left a stamp on our family that was hard to erase—until we left the country for good, that is.

Most of the parents in Puschchino (our town) were scientists and gung ho on their children's education, which was the only way to respectability, especially for those of us who were Jews, actively discriminated against for our background by the state. Of all the many peoples and tribes under the Soviet umbrella, only Jews were singled out for their nationality as *Jewish* in their passports.

There were unwritten, but universally known and strict quotas on Jewish admission to universities and grad schools. Candidates were routinely subjected to graduate testing for undergraduate admissions and otherwise humiliating and arbitrary *rules*. As such, both my parents had to find backdoor ways into doing their PhDs. My father never finished his, but mom defended hers successfully just days before I was born.

I entered school at 5 ½. There I was, on the first day of first grade, September 1, 1988, wearing my navy school uniform with the red scarf, pledging allegiance to the Soviet Union—and my teacher, Yelena Nikolayevna. That year, two Americans came to visit us, one of them African American. Having never seen anyone darkskinned until then, I was shocked and amazed, like all the other kids. Many years later, I learned that a veritable African prince had proposed to Mom at university.

My sister was in 10th grade and graduated that year. Unlikely as it sounds, my Russian language skills were strong enough in 1st grade that for my sister to give me her essays for correction. That was the extent of my practical overlap with Gen X, until a much later age.

The Soviet Union fell when I was 8. Within a couple months, we went from standing in line for hours for staples like bread and milk to suddenly having a glut of Western foods in the stores, just like in the movie

"Goodbye, Lenin." In that initial rush of post-Soviet uncertainty, Mom got an offer to start work right away at the University of Kentucky or at Thomas Jefferson University in 6 months.

Wanting to make a better future for us, partly economic and partly to get us out of an anti-Semitic environment, mom took the Kentucky job ASAP and we took our first flight from Moscow to JFK. We landed in Lexington, Kentucky, on November 5, 1992, the day Bill Clinton was elected president.

There is a distinct memory I have of us getting picked up by mom's new boss, Peter, and his lovely wife, Faye. They took us to McDonald's on the way home and readily gave us dishes, towels, and other home goods to help us get started in our new apartment on the university campus within days.

In the apartment complex, there were other immigrants from all over the world, including most commonly from China, all over Eastern Europe, and even Ireland. In the first 3 months, we had to walk a few miles in the winter cold to Kroger, the local grocery store. As all Soviet immigrants, we were absolutely shocked to see perfect-looking fruits and vegetables in winter, as well as a massive choice of every kind of food, drink, and consumer good.

My sister joined us on a visit from Moscow after 3 months, whereupon mom decisively tore up her return ticket to my sister's tears and hysterics. After a year with us, being 9 years older and already long independent, she relocated to New York to attend the Fashion Institute of Technology (FIT). One early sunny afternoon, the three of us were confronted on the way back from the food co-op by a neo-Nazi who somehow figured out we were Jews, despite the lack of any outward signs (save for the Russian language). The United States had suddenly turned out to be something short of utopia with streets paved in gold.

After being viewed from passing cars like aliens, we finally bought our first car, a refurbished 1989 Dodge Aries. Mom's first job paid $22K, which was a huge salary compared with Soviet wages. We took long drives to neighboring states, especially enjoying the national parks.

While it took some time to understand that Peter and Faye were Mormons gently pushing us to explore the Church of Latter Day Saints, we eventually politely declined, saying that we were Jews and uninterested.

We learned the hard way not argue with missionaries at the door after a couple of drawn-out sessions.

I was placed in fifth grade, because that's where I'd been last in the Russian school system, which was then *modernizing* from grades 10 to 12. I was 9 and by far the youngest kid in class. After a couple of months of English as a Second Language (ESL), I got out and never looked back. I got picked on by a girl much larger than me, who mom said was in love with me. I often walked home through a forest and a large field, with no one any the wiser. Luckily, Child Services never found out, since I came home and stayed alone every day until mom got home from work.

In summer school, I met my oldest friend in America, an Iranian-American named Mehyar. Others would follow from Thailand, Nepal, Vietnam, Ukraine, Israel, and elsewhere. By high school, with a ton of young refugees from Yugoslavia now making their home in town, our class had 22 countries represented.

In seventh grade, I was the best student in language arts, where we learned reams of Latin and Greek roots, which serve me even today. Math and science were always my strong suits.

Being quiet and bookish by nature, I got my As, read my books, played chess, listened to classical and jazz, and largely avoided pop culture. We owned a TV, and at one point, I snuck in Chicago Cubs games, National Basketball Association (NBA), even football games. In Kentucky, the religion being basketball (Go Wildcats!), I quickly learned not just to play (I'd make all kinds of insane, improbable shots from far away), but also all about the different players and coaches and other college teams, then the National Football League (NFL), and Major League Basenall (MLB), even NASCAR, the National Association for Stock Car Auto Racing. Soccer was for playing with other immigrants. I became a bookish nerd with an unnerving memory for player names, stats, and weird facts, which has stuck.

In middle school, I was a model student and mostly kept to myself. The strongest memories I have are of learning etiquette in Mrs. Sims' English class, being the best student in Ms. Ruebling's Spanish class, loving those Latin and Greek roots, as well being sent to detention for unfortunately being grouped with two disruptive troublemakers who managed to insult the teacher, Mrs. Sogin.

When I was 11 or 12, mom got in touch with a local synagogue at one point and I learned in 1 year to become a bar mitzvah. It was a toned down affair, with a few friends attending the *party* with music in the social hall afterward. I bought a bike from Walmart, which lasted me well until the end of high school.

Outside of class, I spent far too much time outside of homework and chores on reading *National Geographic, Microsoft Encarta,* and playing *Where in the World is Carmen Sandiego?* on our Gateway 2000 computer. The first CDs I got as a free bonus by mail order, to my mom's protestations, were Green Day's *Dookie* and REM's *Monster.* I could finally sort of relate to the music taste of the *"real Americans"* in my class.

We moved around from apartment complex to apartment complex a few times until I was around 15, which feels like the time when everything sort of went into overdrive. Right before my birthday, I got the idea in my mind that we *must* buy a house, despite mom's worries about her job and our finances. I pushed the mortgage process as far as I could on my own, effectively, to get her to sign the papers and give over the relevant checks.

After just 5 years, we had achieved a big part of the American Dream, homeownership. I remember planting a Japanese maple in the front yard and feeling pretty proud of my persuasive ability. We would soon apply for citizenship and get sworn in, renouncing our allegiance to any sovereign king, dictator, and so on. Good riddance.

School wasn't terribly taxing. I did just enough to get all As, with the one exception being . . . Health class (yes, health class). I corrected it later through a correspondence course. Mom actually wrote a note exempting me from the Sex Ed portion, which I sat out for a couple of weeks in the school library—such were Soviet social mores around the subject, with the famous phrase, "There is no sex in the Soviet Union," a stock joke after the first—and most famous—Soviet–American tele-bridge in 1986.

One portion of health class I'll never forget was part of abstinence-only education mandated in Kentucky then. Our school ordered electronic, life-size babies that cried every 2 hours for 2 weeks. The episode I remember best is riding my bike in the rain to my French lesson at the University of Kentucky and having the baby cry like crazy in my backpack. I had to stop in the pouring rain, in full view of the drive-by gawkers, and *feed* the baby by inserting a key into its back for a few minutes.

(I happily confirm that this approach did little to dampen my enthusiasm for marriage or kids, even if it hardly gave any realistic sense of just how hard it is in the first few years of raising real-life kids.)

Sometime in sophomore year, I was so naively miffed about being offered drugs outside of school that one day I went on WhiteHouse.gov and wrote a message to President Clinton about the distasteful situation. I was somewhat shocked to find a letter from the White House a few weeks later, commending me on my commitment against drugs on school grounds or some other such boilerplate nonsense. *No doubt* about it, Slick Willy himself had signed it, I quickly realized in my default cynicism. But hey, immigrant kid gets a letter from the White House. That's got to count for something, right? (And all I got was this threadbare DARE t-shirt, LOL.)

In the middle of senior year, the tech bubble burst and the storm-in-a-teacup of Y2K went pass, largely unnoticed.

In school, I was always busy with extracurricular activities. Academic Team was my main squeeze, together with future Jeopardy contestants, Googlers, PhDs, and fellow knowledge-thirsty travelers. I rose to captain of Junior Varsity, then Varsity in senior year. Otherwise, there was Chess club, Beta Club, National Honor Society, Student Council, and a few others I can't recall. For the Senior Yearbook Benefit, I wrote a comic skit—presciently for our current time, it turned out.

The skit lampooned a Russian *conspiracy* that had us getting A's in English and in Math (LOL, we actually did), with me at its head, together with two fellow Russians (*Igor Igorovich*, now a surgeon and *Boris Borisovich*, a consultant) and my Iranian friend (a neurologist) involved. Two Americans were also part of the group, a John (a Princeton and University of Virginia grad in private equity) and a Jimbo (an environmentalist). The crowning moment was getting our U.S. history teacher, Mr. Pope, involved as the righteous American who comes to break up our conspiracy and whom I asked in a Russian brogue, "Put up your dukes, as they say," upon which he chased us off stage with an American flag.

As a thank you gift at graduation, a mere couple of weeks after Columbine upended school security with cameras now all over the school, but no officers yet stationed inside, I brought in a shoebox with a hammer and a sickle to school, tied with a red thread, which I gave to Mr. Pope.

He still has it in his garage all these years later, he texted me recently. Now imagine how differently life would have turned out if I'd gotten arrested for such a joke today!

Boy, those were simpler, happier times—before smartphone addiction, before schools were shot up almost daily, when the gerontocracy still sort of cared about governing through consensus, before life was lived in anxiety on social media, before privacy was lost forever, and before everyone had to sell and brand themselves constantly. For that alone, as an *old* millennial or Xennial, I will always be grateful.

I did come out of my shell toward the end of senior year, even giving a speech to 5,000 people at the famed Rupp Arena at our graduation. I went to prom with my first *girlfriend* from synagogue, whom I'd known since 12 or so. My look in the pictures was truly cringeworthy, awkward in the best American tradition of prom pictures.

After graduation, I was headed to UPenn for undergrad. We moved to Baltimore for mom's transferred job mere days after graduation. After two summers of doing neuroscience research with mom in her lab during high school, I continued in her new lab in Baltimore.

Starting college at Penn was a revelation. From the first day, I quickly found all sorts of fascinating people, starting with my dorm, which looked like a half-modern, half-medieval moated fortress— Hill House, a former women's dorm with no AC. My roommate was a Taiwanese guy from Saudi Arabia (now a patent lawyer). One was a half-Lithuanian, half-Romanian Jewish Canuck, who became a dear friend and now runs an amazing nonprofit in Montreal. Another was a half-Chilean, half-Swiss fireball of a girl, also a close friend, who became a war-zone journalist and who lived in my neighborhood in New York after graduation.

There were prep school kids from both coasts; a Brunei prince who threw a birthday party in a club downtown in the first week; frat brothers and sorority sisters; Russians from Brighton Beach, who seemed like instant friends from a foreign world; kids from all over Europe, Latin America, Africa, plus from all over the United States—future bankers, doctors, law partners, PhDs, start-up CEOs, business leaders, policymakers, marketers, you name it. Back then, we were just kids starting out on our respective journeys.

And there I was, a scholarship kid from a lower-middle-class, single-parent immigrant family, finally released into the intellectual wild with brilliant professors and ultra-sharp, motivated kids. A premed by intent, but harboring not-so-secret literary ambitions, I had quickly bitten off more than I could chew, class-wise. With a year and change in college credits from Advanced Placement (AP), used to doing just the minimum for an A in high school, I was quickly disheartened by competing with prep school kids with a serious and far superior work ethic, trained from their Stuyvesant or Bronx Science or Andover days for the long haul.

After the first semester, there was no illusion of all As, as I barely eked out a B average. Over the next four semesters, I would complete an unprecedented downward slide, beyond mediocrity toward downright perdition, dropping below a B average and having my study abroad in Seville cancelled last minute. Although I'd decided on Biological Basis of Behavior (basically, neuroscience) as a major, most of it was premed courses.

My layered learning style, which meant in practice that I learned more slowly, but meaningfully in concert with other disciplines, looking for connections between concepts and fields, had clearly proven too slow and suboptimal for the gorge-and-regurgitate expectations of premed courses. I wasn't out of my depth, as much as I was just not a good fit for the mass-produced, mass-consumption learning culture of medicine.

Einstein's quote about a fish judged for climbing trees comes to mind. In fact, it would come to define both my undergraduate and graduate school experiences.

Even as the sh*t continued to hit the fan over and over, with greater and greater gravity and coverage area for my future, I wasted little time in looking for a group of kids I could relate to. Most turned out to be either international misfits with voracious appetites for knowledge or straight-laced Wharton students from my background.

Both neatly came together in a semisecret literary and debate group I'd joined, called The Philomathean Society, around continuously until today, since 1813. During a November meeting to select the members of the next class (which never officially happened, ehem), I went out in the hallway of College Hall to release some energy after sitting for 2 hours. I jumped up to touch the high doorway and landed awkwardly, seeing my left wrist assume an unnatural shape.

As the doctor confirmed, I'd broken both bones. But worse than the injury itself, with surgery and a cast, plus the loss of use of an arm for a few weeks, was the insult of being foolish enough to rely on myself (Soviet style) to continue all my errands, work–study job, plus full class load. Having no habit to ask for help, or at least to utilize it when it was available, I worked my way right into a handful of Cs and Ds and nearly burned out from the premed rigamarole.

And so, there I was, hitting bottom with a B average, no longer going on subsidized debauchery in Spain for a semester, back home, tail between my legs. Med school was by now an impossibility. At that point, I hated Philly, hated Penn, and was by and large disgusted and unmoored. At least there was still a path into a PhD program, given my lab research experience and excellent references.

For the spring semester, I decided to get away from premed and neuroscience, stopping one class short of Organic Chemistry Lab, the crown jewel of premed misery. Instead, I took an amazing combination of physical anthropology, 20th Century German Literature, History of Romance Languages, and other humanities courses. It was my best semester to date, by far. My good humor began to return. Around that time, I was forced to get a cell phone when my Greyhound bus arrived super late to New York from Baltimore, causing my mom and sister to worry overly.

Several friendships deepened that remain until this day. One of them turned romantic after an inebriated conversation at a party, whereupon I briefly wore her heels (and didn't fall down). Given her soon-to-be Peace Corps assignment in Ghana, home to my namesake Kruman tribe, I nicknamed her West Africa. Her father wrote for the *New Yorker* and was a Princeton historian. We were total opposites in terms of politics, worldview, and on the optimism/pessimism axis. As relationships tend to do in college, it burned bright and fast. I ran into her briefly, years later, on a subway platform in New York, eliciting a shocked pause before the doors closed.

When mom was up to Philly in April for my birthday, on a riverside walk by the art museum, I distinctly remember a tourist asking where the zoo was. I half-jokingly barked back, "What, not enough animals around?" Right around that time, a new site called Facebook.com came online at Penn and I joined.

While I could have graduated after 3, even 2 ½ years, and gone to grad school, one of the best decisions I ever made was to stay the full 4 years. I experienced tremendous growth as a human and these experiences stay with me to this day.

Purely for context, the most famous classmate of mine was none other than Ivanka Trump. Less famous, but still quite impressive was a group of classmates who started and sold Venmo. The rest of us were mostly still preprofessional, aspiring entrepreneurs, Teach for America material, Peace Corps volunteers, or about to "kill it" on Wall Street.

So that was it for college, and I moved back home to Baltimore for a couple of months before next steps.

Bright eyed and bushy tailed, I felt ready to take on the world and thrilled to be in New York City. While I had toyed with the ideas of going to Israel for law school and also with doing a PhD in anthropology, going to work in the *real world* hardly entered my mind. Such was my upbringing that neuroscience was the first stop on a career in the field.

And so, the next step took me to New York University's Sackler School of Biomedical Graduate Studies on a (supposedly prestigious) neuroscience training grant.

After a brief interlude, which I used to go on a Birthright trip to Israel for 10 days, I moved with mom's help into a grad student dorm in Manhattan's Murray Hill neighborhood. There, college grads from all the same colleges and high schools conspired to *work hard, play hard*, while us grad students pretended to do the same.

The world seemed full of possibility when I arrived right after July 4 in 2004 to start my neuroscience Ph.D. program.

That is, with a notable caveat the size of Mammoth Cave. While I had undoubtedly received a world-class education that millions of people would kill for (for which I will be eternally grateful), the simple, unvarnished truth is that nowhere throughout my 4 years in an Ivy League institution did I learn (or was required or encouraged to learn) the most important life skills that underpin professional and financial success in the modern economy.

These include career management, financial management (how to live within your means, budgeting, and loan repayment), time management, copywriting, personal branding, or starting a business. But alas, those skills would be earned much later, out of distress and few options, rather than preemptively.

Whatever your reaction may be, whether it's *should have just gone to business school* or *burden's on you, buddy*, unless you're a millennial yourself, odds are that your first thought was, *damned, entitled millennial.*

There is some truth in this, no doubt, but with a big wrinkle. It's easy to demonize the young for making mistakes when one is safely insulated from one's own youthful mistakes by years, status, experience and/or selective amnesia. It's much easier to blame younger generations for failing than to take responsibility for remedying your failure to give them the requisite life skills.

Imagine blaming aspiring law students for believing law school employment percentages advertised in the high 90s. If your parents are both lawyers and you miss the fine print, shame on you and your parents. But if you have no one in your family or networks to help you cut through the bullsh*tBS to the truth behind the marketing, then shame on the law school and its law guild enablers.

But I digress.

In my year in the PhD program, I had a jolly old time socially, making new friends at will, carousing at the old Mehanata with Bulgarians and making other mischief. The program itself was interesting, but hardly engaging for me. It was a bad fit all around.

In my second lab rotation, where the head of the lab (whose daughter was a top model) had once gone down south to help desegregation in the '60s, I hit a wall. Whereas I was expected to be in lab 24/7, I failed to show up more than twice over the course of a month. Instead, I spent nearly the whole month in the dorm, depressed and making excuses for my absence, even while I was building the first Jewish social network, which I called JuicyJews.com.

One notable event from that time in my life was a brief and awkward date, punctuated by a mild tremor from Viennese coffee on an empty stomach, with the beleaguered daughter of the (in)famous Dr. Zismor (unfortunately nicknamed "Zits-more") of New York subway fame for 30 years, who would for the life of her not tell me her last name when we connected on JDate. Using my sleuthing skills, I figured it out anyway. Ten hours of over-caffeination later, I finally managed to get to sleep.

As for JuicyJews.com, I'd spent my entire savings of $3,000 for guys in India to code it (and not very well). The site launched to a spike of traffic from Facebook, where I'd effectively built the first global group (under a profile called *Judah the Maccabi*), and promptly died. I still have t-shirts with the logo in a closet, as a reminder.

I'd failed spectacularly, yet again. A few months later, I was politely asked to leave the program by its head, whose neurophysiology lab I was in at that point. Bad grades were one thing, but being asked to leave was another kind of failure, altogether. The disappointment of my mom that I'd never become a colleague was heavy and persistent (even to this day).

But the show had to go on. So I pulled myself together, moved into another apartment nearby with a college friend from Panama and began a series of *real-world* jobs/projects starting with selling office supplies for W.B. Mason, followed by paralegal gigs for Paul Weiss, Pfizer, plus a couple of other large law firms. Meanwhile, I took the Law School Admissions Test (LSAT), scored half-decently, applied and got into several solid schools. Best among them was my choice, Cardozo.

Once more, not having budgeting or financial management skills, I was ill-equipped for life as anything but a projected, highly paid attorney at graduation.

Law school was anything but enjoyable, a succession of classes where I was a middling student, at best, and a reluctant intern in my various internships during the semesters and summers. I often skipped class to write my first novel at a coffee shop. Great way to spend $250K I didn't have and ruin the next 10 years of my life, I know. Most of that debt at 8.5 percent, otherwise at 6.5 percent and 5 percent, depending in the loan. Can I hear you say, FML?

The internships ranged from insurance defense litigation for a firm that fired me on my last day (yes, you read that correctly; they were shamelessly trying to save on paying my rate for a couple days) to legal consulting (essentially lawyer triage for high-level politicians, celebrities, and others for a former adviser to New York governors and mayors, working from her 5th Avenue apartment, with lunches at Daniel) and a personal injury and medical malpractice firm where I was the *Associates* and recorded a commercial that ran for months on Russian primetime TV and made me recognizable to Russian-speaking cabbies around the city. LOL, Russian pride.

The personal injury lawyer paid me reasonably well, let me go to Israel on a fellowship for 17 days, and even set me up in a sort of corner office in the Woolworth building with a stunning view of the Hudson and New Jersey. As life would have it, 9 years later, I would be back *exactly* in the same room, with my pregnant wife for a checkup at her gynecologist, who'd recently changed offices.

But the personal injury lawyer did extract his pound of flesh without me knowing, using my law school logins to LexisNexis and WestLaw, a fact I learned from a friend who interned with him right after me.

My last internship, which I found myself through a friend and for which I got school credit, was in *legal/compliance* at a London-based hedge fund. I commuted 90 minutes each way by train twice a week and witnessed as Bear Stearns went under, Wachovia was swallowed up, and 401(k) s and all sorts of investments got a massive haircut overnight, with our financial system suddenly on the brink of seeming collapse. The fund would soon close its New York office and retrench in London.

Exciting times! I suddenly found finance as an intellectual topic to be of great interest.

Come graduation, I'd barely managed a B-/C+ average. Bar prep was an awful drag, and I had to take out another $15K for that summer, for the bar prep course and to support myself while studying.

I'd moved in with a friend from a wealthy family into an apartment that was too expensive, in the vague hopes of finding a job quickly. This was 2009, mind you, still at the high point of the Great Recession, when the traditional legal business model was falling apart and a massive swath of legal jobs simply evaporated overnight.

Come early November, at the funeral of my ex-girlfriend's grandfather, I got the e-mail that I'd failed the New York bar exam. A few days later, at the airport on my mom's birthday after flying to see her for a few days, New Jersey obliged with similar news.

This was a whole new level of embarrassment, dejection, hopelessness, and lack of direction. It also meant I had to move back in immediately with mom in Lubbock, Texas, with my tail between my legs and a surreal sense that I'd screwed up my whole life, both professional and social.

I was a grown-ass man at 26, feeling sorry for myself as an unqualified failure, despite an Ivy League bachelors and a law degree, high IQ, plus the impossible expectations of my family, girlfriend, and friends.

Aside from a friend who sent me a package of kosher beef jerky to cheer me up and invited me to live with him in his tiny Manhattan studio for a few months while I got back on my feet, I felt isolated, alone, and shattered. Being with mom at home again, suddenly the little boy and giant disappointment, I couldn't just hang around for long without going crazy, G-d bless mom.

I quickly reached my threshold for parental input, and within 2 months, moved back to New York in January 2010 to stay half the week on one friend's couch on Upper East Side and another's in Astoria.

To bring in some sort of revenue while I waited to retake the bar exam, I helped a doctor off Craigslist put together his self-represented case in counter-suing several large insurance companies for millions in unpaid claims. He paid me an hourly rate and promised a cut of the winnings.

Crazy enough, largely on the back of my legal strategy, drafting, and argumentation skills on paper against an army of health insurance defense litigators, he actually did manage to win a couple of the cases, but swore off promising me any cut of anything. It was yet one more in a long string of desperate gigs to bring in revenue that led to disappointment, getting screwed, and feeling powerless to fight back.

A few weeks after my return to New York, my girlfriend of 4 ½ years, whom I was ready to marry *as soon as* a job and stability materialized, broke up with me and shattered what seemed like the last great hope in my life.

With a little help from my friends, I bounced back as quickly as I could. Little did I know, I'd already met my wife at a Jewish event on a major holiday.

In April, I found a gig through a recruiter, doing legal/compliance at Fortress Investment Group, a major hedge fund. That was actually an amazing experience, learning a ton about real estate and credit fund operations from my boss and colleagues.

In early June, I went on my first date with my now-wife after hot-listing her on JDate and finding out I'd already met her. Neither of us had a permanent place to live, but we most certainly saw eye to eye about raising a family, not dating forever before marriage, and a range of other subjects. That was, despite being from wildly different backgrounds, with completely different educations and worldviews.

After barely 2 months, with her gone on a world-wide trip to see her far-flung family members, I picked her up as a surprise from the airport. A week later, while we were having drinks, I got an e-mail from a friend moving out of her highly coveted and majorly subsidized, under-the-table Columbia Housing apartment to live with her soon-to-be-husband, another friend. She wanted to keep the apartment among friends and we both jumped at the chance.

A week later, we both moved in our stuff from storage and started our life together. A few days later, I bought an engagement ring, proposed in a garden under the Brooklyn Bridge, and we were legally husband and wife at City Hall, with two friends as witnesses, within 2 weeks. Oh, and my now-wife had also lost her work visa, so the timing worked couldn't have been better.

As we started planning for our religious wedding the next June, my wife raised concerns about my awful finances, with sky-high debt and lack of a safe, full-time job now yet more pressing. We almost called it off at one point, but made it work and kept going.

The Fortress gig ended with the year. Two months later, I was on a new gig doing compliance at Goldman Sachs's Jersey office, "the largest phallus in New Jersey" (as I phrased it in my novel). Mind numbing and stressful as the job itself was, at least, it gave me excellent material for my novel. That ended after just 2 months.

Our wedding was a month later. With prayers and a bit of luck, I talked my way into my first ever *permanent*, full-time job as a credit risk analyst at a medium-sized bank, Brown Brothers Harriman. My boss, an Oxford Brit and archconservative, ran a tight ship in our department, leveraging British understatement and passive-aggressiveness to make understanding his true intent difficult, if not impossible.

While at Brown Brothers, I started a company with a health tech investor friend to attempt underwriting health insurance from a tech perspective. We called it More Spinach, Inc. Like most early start-ups, but more, we had an exaggerated chicken-and-egg problem with getting funding without users and trying to get users without funding, since to apply or buy insurance licenses took millions of dollars we didn't have.

As a side note, throughout the 3 years following graduation, I was still doing bar prep and took the bar exam three more times, failing three more times to mounting frustration from my wife and disappointment from my mom. It was patently clear that I simply wasn't meant to be a practicing lawyer, since my heart and mind weren't in it, but my family took much longer to accept the obvious.

Back on the start-up front, at one point, I even suggested a plan for Brown Brothers to save money by adjusting their health plans, which was received well and awarded with . . . a BBH mug written up in permanent marker.

I held on for a year and 2 months at Brown Brothers until the axe came. Keeping face when you hate your work, find it meaningless, and are not given a way to express yourself or see a hint of care in your direction became impossible for me. And so, on that day in August, while I was mortified to come home and tell my wife, I paradoxically felt immense relief that I was leaving.

We closed down More Spinach a few months later, but I had at least made inroads into health tech. A full eight incredibly stressful, frustrating months passed in between with thousands of resumes and e-mails sent to no effect. The same friend whose beef jerky I'd happily eaten and whose couch I'd once stayed on invited me to a Jewish early morning prayer group, so I could meet a noted career coach and get his input for free.

That gentleman, Ira Ziff, a well-known Wall Street recruiter and career coach, changed my life with a quick look over my resume and detailed suggestions for how to change my resume and LinkedIn profile to tell my story more clearly, concisely, and effectively. To him, I owe much more than just my first six-figure gig (a credit risk project at Bank of America), which I got shortly thereafter and started days before turning 30, thus achieving an important goal of mine.

Ira showed me that he cared enough to help out a desperate kid with a family who had nothing to pay or give him in return. He also showed me that coaching is an incredibly powerful and useful thing for the person being helped, as well as for the coach him- or herself. I had been cured of my Soviet self-reliance syndrome and saw that simply asking someone for help had actually led to much better results than I could hope to achieve on my own, at least within a reasonable time. And thus, the maxim, *If you don't ask, the answer is always no*, became a mantra.

The changes kept coming. Three days before I started my new role, my wife was laid off from her large tech company, 2 weeks after announcing she was pregnant. When I came to get her by end of day, she was crying and incredibly upset. I assured her we'd be laughing shortly because of the company's legal ineptitude, and helped her gather all the documents as proof that they'd fired her for being pregnant. My legal training had come in quite useful, at last!

Sure enough, mere weeks after she was fired, with the help of a top employment lawyer and family friend, she reached a hefty settlement with them for a year's worth of salary and benefits. For the first time, I was (sort of, kind of) the breadwinner for the family. Hooray.

Around the same time, when my wife and I visited Morocco, I made a decision to try bargaining in earnest for the first time in my life. Having nothing to lose, I bargained with a guy in the souk and got the (dramatically lower) price I'd asked for. While it seemed like a humorous trifle for my wife's Moroccan family, who grew up negotiating from birth, for me it was nothing short of a paradigm shift from which I've never looked back.

Back home in New York, we got ready for our first kid after trying for 2 years. My first novel got to the printers quickly after I raised $5K on Kick starter to publish it, thanks to our dear and generous friends. I had also won a Blueprint Fellowship for the project that became my second book (a shorter novella).

In short succession, our daughter was born in late September 2013 and my first book was published and launched days later. My Bank of America project sadly ended with the year, as did the Blueprint Fellowship, with my second book published in January 2014. And so, I stayed at home while looking for a new gig, taking our daughter to a baby gym for the Papa's version of "Mommy & Me" after my wife started her new job in mid-spring, post–maternity leave.

While it was yet another time full of stress, calls, meetings, and sending of resumes, never mind reconfiguring of traditional gender roles, in retrospect, it was one of the most fun and enjoyable times of my life. I still have in my phone notes when Leora first laughed, when she first walked, spoke her first word ("Amen" in response to a blessing). We walked/strolled all over Manhattan, flew with her to France, Morocco, and Israel before she was 3 months old. It was a magic and precious time that I will always remember.

Yet, with the months passing without an offer, the pressure built up. We closed More Spinach and wound it down. In the spring, I finally got traction on one opportunity, when an entrepreneurial HR director (now a friend, originally from Afghanistan, by way of Kansas) took a chance on me and hired me into his healthcare Big Data consulting company after I passed behavioral and case interviews simply by preparing, despite zero prior experience with consulting.

My first (and turns out, only) project took me to a large public retirement fund, where I was on a project for a whopping month, to rave reviews. In my third week, I got a call from the (Gen X) CEO of a Venture Capital (VC)-backed health care benefits Software-as-a-Service (SaaS) start-up I'd been talking to since More Spinach was just starting. On paper, our worldviews aligned and I loved the mission and (stated) values of the company he was building. We'd spoken on and off for 18 months until then, in person and by phone.

He asked me to join him for lunch the next day. While chowing down on Korean, he told me he was unhappy with his director of finance (should have set off my alarm bells, already) and needed someone to come in underneath him, learn everything, and then replace the director. I mentioned again that I was interested in product management and had zero experience in finance and operations.

He asked me a series of questions about my ability to deal with contracts (that law degree coming in useful); read and manage a financial model, cash flow statements, and balance sheets; help with BizDev, investor relations, and other high-level tasks. I answered quite forthrightly that I'm a quick learner and trusted my ability to ramp up quickly.

He offered me a job and $15K more right on the spot, asking me to be in Boston for the company retreat the next morning. I made it work and asked him to make it a full-time offer with benefits, which he did. He even had me stay with him in the same hotel room, unloading further on his director of finance, an MBA with solid finance experience. And so, I basically walked in off the street to a 50-person start-up to help manage finance and operations, having drunk the entire stock of Kool-Aid.

The company was a truly cool, young, hip start-up with offices in New York and Boston, offering excellent benefits, a fully stocked kitchen, and other Google-like perks. There was an open floor plan, talented people, amazing mission, cool offices, free coffee and snacks, unlimited vacation. According to the CEO, the director and I were considered equals and colleagues, with the eventual plan being for me to replace the director.

On paper, this was millennial heaven. In practice, it meant micro-managed hell, insane hours, and expectations. A month into the job, the director left for a full month to India, leaving me to manage the financial model, contracts, payroll, employee on-boarding, the monthly close, in-vestor relation document prep, and everything else under his purview. To say I was overwhelmed doesn't nearly do justice. After he got back from his trip, the pressure ratcheted up. Four to five months in, I was really struggling and barely staying afloat. Plans suddenly changed, and I was made the director's direct report. After a couple months, I was simply burned out. One day, I was unceremoniously let go. On my way out, I told the director how his head has been on the chopping block all along. Months later, the director also left because of awful treatment; a CFO came and left after a month and it was clear something was rotten in start-up Denmark.

Meanwhile, I managed to cold-e-mail and talk my way into a senior product manager (PM) role at a larger competitor, despite nothing but basic experience as a PM, beating the noncompete from the previous company. It sounds like something between a silver tongue and amazing luck at play, but to be perfectly frank, it was desperation and resourceful-ness to get a job that propelled me. The interviewing and negotiation had already been baked into my approach, and I bumped up my starting pay by $10K with a couple of quick e-mails.

I started after a few weeks on a team of highly experienced product managers with MBAs from Harvard, Stanford, Northwestern, and the like. No pressure, right? That also didn't go over well. It was survival mode almost from the start, piled onto implicit hostility to an upstart like my-self. I was out of there in 5 months, a patently bad fit.

One more tailspin, more harsh conversations with my wife about my future, *our* future. On top of all the stress about paying back loans (I'd just started the snowball method since starting as a PM, but now had to stop repayment again and resume a mix of deferment and forbearance on my loans) to make ends meet, pay for day care and other basic expenses.

At this time, my best friend told me about an early-stage start-up whose pitch he'd heard at work, run by a guy I (thought I) knew well from college. Great Wall Street, Israeli Army pedigree, great salesman, partnered with an Ivy League doctor, plus all the rest. When I connected with the CEO, I wanted to work with him and in short order was made a Director, which wasn't worth its salt. I also invested $10K of our money and got a handful of friends to invest a total of $160K in the start-up (which is still dragging along with no employees and cash running out, despite rave reviews and great service).

At first, I was formally a contractor for a pittance and worthless equity, working from home. Then, I was made a full-time employee, commuting into an office back in Manhattan. That February, we'd moved to Brooklyn after our under-the-table Columbia Housing apartment was taken from our hands at the renter's death in Puerto Rico (we never did meet him). Rent shot up by more than a factor of two. Miraculously, I'd managed to pass the credit check with the new job *just* formalized.

At that time, I started driving an Uber clone (no longer in existence[1]) called CliqCar, a semisecret offshoot of Gett Car. As a writer, the experience was most fascinating, if ultimately useless for any meaningful revenue over the course of 4 months or so, despite working a couple of 10-hour shifts twice a week after commuting into midtown and back. It very nearly screwed up my health, since I was in the start-up job simultaneously.

A couple of months in, our younger daughter was born. Health care was paid by the start-up, not my wife, at this point. When our daughter was 2 months old, her pediatrician discovered something wrong during a routine checkup, sending us to one, then another specialist at Sloan Kettering. He'd found a cancerous mass, stage 3B, one short of metastasis into the brain. I was having trouble at work again, this time because I was challenging the CEO's mis-steps (like the other employees, just more vocally). I was pushed out once more. The CEO refused to extend health

---

[1] For fuller story, see https://thoughtcatalog.com/yuri-kruman/2016/06/driving-a-taxi-is-the-new-black/.

coverage despite our daughter's diagnosis. Again, I was unemployed and sh*t out of luck. My wife and I were both at an edge and had terrible fights that seemed to be leading in only one direction.

The world seemed to be falling, even much harder than with everything else on our shoulders. In the middle of this, we decided I would focus on coaching and start-up consulting full time, while staying at home with our daughter and taking care of the older one, as well.

While starting a business is never easy, doing so with zero margin for error to keep one's family whole and after four careers that didn't work out, raised the stakes as high as they could possibly go. It was heady stuff, but for the first time in my career, I truly felt a *click* in that I was helping people by adding massive value to their lives, building a business on my own that leveraged my own crazy story of multiple career changes, two failed start-ups, massive setbacks and challenges to actually help people switch careers, grow their businesses, and otherwise find their life mission.

I also started telling my story, with all the unvarnished failures and dead ends, to anyone who would listen. I lost my shame and stopped giving a damn about what anyone thought. There was no longer any career escalator or rat race to worry about. No more trying to be everyone to everybody and ending up a nobody to everyone. This was true bottom, with only the stars above.

We pushed through the health coverage issue, switching the insurance to my wife's company to pay for the series of chemo treatments (10, in total), costing a quaint $20K a pop. Our family and community supported us incredibly well, helping with child care, prayers, and every other way they could. Our daughter started getting better with the treatments, although after a relapse, we were afraid they'd have to do a surgical removal. We also took her every Friday for a number of weeks to an energy healer, a PhD in statistics and professor, of all things. We prayed and said Psalms regularly, anything to prevent remission.

Needless to say, our faith and marriage were both mightily tested with all the emotional and diagnostic ups and downs and early morning visits to Sloan Kettering's floor for children, along with the challenges of building a business.

Nevertheless, thank G-d, both of us and our marriage emerged much stronger. We were incredibly fortunate to be in the city with the world's topmost expert for the specific cancer. We caught it in the nick of time. We didn't have to surgically remove anything. We had insurance coverage thanks to my wife's work. We had a supportive community to help us through the ordeal, even as our family lives 5+ hours away by plane. Things could have turned out much differently, but thank G-d, they turned out well. And for that, we're all incredibly grateful.

We persevered and our little one beat the cancer after 14 months of treatments. She still gets checkups every couple of months, plus a small treatment or two, but we're thankfully past the worst.

And that brings us to today. With all the challenges and setbacks as the background, I've managed to grow the business through a few dramatic ups and downs and pivots and greater focus and understanding into a corporate consulting/executive coaching/start-up advising shop with features and mentions in many top publications, podcasts, TV shows, and others.

In this relatively short 2.5 years, I've helped 300+ mid-career millennial execs to transform their careers, build successful side businesses, and otherwise meaningfully improve their career and life trajectories. In addition, I've done all my own sales, PR, coaching, consulting, marketing, and everything in between. None of this would have been possible without my incredible—and incredibly patient—wife, my rock.

There is no magic rags-to-riches story here, just continued hard work, measured optimism, and measured progress in the face of massive challenges. If you wake up in the morning, say thank you to the Almighty and your loved ones and do your best with what you have, to make things better for others and yourself.

The best is surely yet to come.

Summary

Personal History as Guide—author's story and how it's uniquely emblematic of the millennial experience, trauma, dislocation, disruption, and decentralization

CHAPTER 3

Millennial Voices

It was the best of times, it was the worst of times, it was the age of wisdom, it was the age of foolishness, it was the epoch of belief, it was the epoch of incredulity, it was the season of Light, it was the season of Darkness, it was the spring of hope, it was the winter of despair, we had everything before us, we had nothing before us, we were all going direct to Heaven, we were all going direct the other way—in short, the period was so far like the present period, that some of its noisiest authorities insisted on its being received, for good or for evil, in the superlative degree of comparison only.

—Charles Dickens, *A Tale of Two Cities*

It's tempting to look for figureheads and *voices of a generation* to laud or blame in good times and in bad, respectively.

Blame the President when the economy goes south. Blame the tech CEO when there's a data breach. Laud the *perfect* millennial who *actually* paid his or her dues on the way to the boardroom. Praise the boomer who's *hip* and on Snapchat.

But blaming or praising, looking up to or denigrating figureheads and famous members of a generation is misguided and shortsighted. Googling *famous millennials* inevitably leads to some mix of tech moguls like Zuckerberg, politicos like Ivanka + Jared and Kim Jong Il, royals such as Prince William, actors like Mila Kunis and Scarlett Johansson, fashion starlets like Kendall Jenner, music icons like Beyonce and Justin Bieber, sports stars like LeBron, Simone Biles, and Michael Phelps, plus inspirational figures like Malala.

Do any of these famous people truly represent millennials? Yes and no, just like the rest of us. Everyone has their struggles, but is there someone whose story is truly emblematic of all the unique struggles, historical milestones, and experiences particular to millennials? Probably not.

Even with all my misadventures, challenges, identity crises, and life and career transitions, I can't claim credit for being some sort of über-millennial, any more than the next guy who's changed a ton of jobs, holds a Fort Knox worth's of school debt, loves his avocado toast, and was a Facebook early adopter.

And as such, the knee-jerk denigration of millennials by Gen X and boomer journalists and talking heads as lazy, flaky, unreliable, smartphone addicted, or anything else (see Chapter 1 for the full laundry list) is nothing but shortsighted and downright ridiculous. It's akin to calling all dogs rabid after a few reports of dogs biting men. And no, wise guy, millennials are not dogs.

Even just anecdotally, I've known millennials both Luddite and smartphone addicted, foodies and bland bores, some flaky and other too loyal to their work, homeowners and apartment dwellers, car owners and never drivers, many social media obsessed and others with zero entries on Google, glamorous and nerdy, ambitious beyond belief and scatterbrained stoners, tolerant of everything and everyone and others completely intolerant bigots, futurists and retrophiles, parents and single forever, socialists and archconservatives, rich and broke to tears, entrepreneurs and paycheck lifers, social butterflies and scared wallflowers, healthy and sick, honest and frauds, brilliant and anything-but, optimists and cynics, with everything in between, in shades.

But I digress.

Why are millennial *voices* not being heard on uniquely millennial issues? More to the point, why aren't there more millennials talking publicly, vocally, and consistently about such issues? Or at least, why aren't there more millennials willing to stick out their neck with principled stands on issues of great importance, other than to register complaints against Trump or climate change denialists?

In an age where it's never been easier to reach a larger audience, more quickly than ever in history (over Twitter, Facebook, Instagram, Snapchat, or other large social media platforms), it is paradoxically difficult to think of millennials actually speaking out politically in a concerted, large-magnitude effort over a meaningfully long period of time.

The closest instance that comes to mind is the concerted, sustained <u>reaction</u> to the Parkland school shooting episode in the form of political protest and lobbying for gun control by those young men and women actually affected. Ironically, these brave kids are actually Gen Z, not millennials. What's the *problem* with today's millennials? Do they feel muzzled? Are they afraid to speak out? What's actually going on here to explain this phenomenon?

It certainly isn't for lack of issues to deal with. Let's start with the impassive, kleptocratic gerontocracy that's our government, the looming student debt, real estate, and a host of other bubbles. There is the issue of millennials being the first American generation worse off than their parents. Then, there is the lingering wage gap for women, the wide and increasing socioeconomic gap between the 1 percent and the rest of us, the cartelization of tech, the unchecked spread of *fake news* and *truthiness* (even of *truth is not truth*), the end of privacy and net neutrality, the increasing speed of change, labor force automation, the massive real-life skills gap for college grads, worsening climate change, the breakdown of the liberal world order giving way to a rising tide of nationalist, tribalist autocracies in the world, the refugee crisis in the Middle East and Europe, the end of American global leadership in the world, and so on and so forth. Phew, the world just seems to be falling apart at the seams, right? Not quite.

So what's the matter with millennials? Don't we have enough problems on our plate to complain about in concert, not least as the largest generation in history? Are we afraid to speak up for some reason, perhaps even spineless, or is something else to blame?

First, life in our current moment in American history is hardly one of total despair, no matter how upset the Trump administration, school debt, or any other pressing life issue may make you.

In most important regards, there's simply never been a better time to be alive in America, despite all the geopolitical, world historical problems preoccupying us. Life expectancy is high and increasing.

Access to inexpensive food is consistent and steady for most people. Education and Internet access may be had for free or cheap in most places, allowing anyone to pick up marketable, monetizable skills easily and quickly from Massive Open Online Courses (MOOCs), free courses, universal library access. It's never been easier, faster, or cheaper to connect with and learn from experts, build a business, meet and collaborate with people, travel the world, work remotely, or reinvent yourself.

That's not to mention the core strengths of our open, democratic society that despite various forms of structural inequality in our economy and all branches of federal government, still rests largely in the Constitution and its many protections, as well as long-standing democratic institutions.

In short, whatever our constant (often justified) collective complaints about less-than-blind justice, lack of representation of certain groups, virulent political polarization, and so on, we have it quite good to live in America, at the least by contrast to most other places in the world where such protections are nonexistent or much weaker.

Beyond the many strong reasons for optimism, the idea that millennials are voiceless is far from the truth. In the last 3 to 5 years alone, there's been an explosion of millennial-run and millennial-focused media platforms both general and niche in scope, including Mic, Mogul, Blavity, Elite Daily, Vox, VICE, Refinery29, BuzzFeed, and Upworthy, to name just a few. Even mainstream media have experimented with millennial-focused and -run segments to attract millennial viewership.

So is it that we're spoiled?

Yes and no. It's quite easy (effortless, really) for most of us to take for granted the freedoms of an open society, the technology readily available to make work and daily life so seamlessly easy, as well as a relatively high standard of life, when most of us are simply unfamiliar with the flip side of things from having grown up in a repressive political system with few charms of modern life.

But this isn't about the universal need for anthropology class or fields trips to the inner city. After all, millennials are the most educated generation of all time.

For starters, millennials are still not old enough or far enough along in their development as people or political animals to field much in terms of meaningful political power or winning candidates for high political office.

Aside from Ivanka Trump and Jared Kushner, by far the highest (unelected, albeit) millennial political officials in the United States, there are no millennial senators and only five congressmen and women, whereas by proportional demographics, there should be 97 (nearly 20 times as much) as of 2018.

The one who has made the most noise to date has been the recent victor of a New York congressional primary, Alexandria Ocasio-Cortez, who knocked off a multiterm incumbent in a shock upset. Congress reelects 95 percent of its incumbents, which is the biggest reason for why so few millennials are in Congress and for why the body as a whole has a miserable 15 percent approval rating.

November 2018 has already brought a sea change. Baby boomers are no longer the largest voting bloc. Ocasio-Cortez's win is expected to be more than just a fluke, with a number of congressional candidates fielded by Democrats and Republicans, alike, now victorious.

The picture is quite different at the local, city hall level, around the country, as millennials have already broken through in many localities, bringing fresh ideas and change, albeit overwhelmingly from the left side of the political spectrum.

In short, whereas old, white men have all but bottled up political, corporate, media, and economic power for themselves for much of the last 40 years, the cracks are widening and the lava's escaping. The eruption's only a matter of time, at most a handful of years.

***

Volcanoes and gerontocracies aside, let's turn our focus to the present and future. Whether or not we're given permission, leverage, room to roam, adult treatment (choose your own metaphor), we simply have no choice—like every generation before millennials going through the same stage—but to take matters into our own hands.

The biggest and best thing we have going for us is simple demographics. While Gen Z is set to overtake millennials shortly as the largest generation, we are primed to enter more boardrooms and halls of power, remake more industries and business models through sheer career momentum, spending power, increasing awareness of just how screwed we are, an acquired resourcefulness, and ubiquitous frustration with the status quo.

Before we delve into the much-hyped power of the blockchain in helping decentralize institutions, work, currencies, contracts, health care, and a host of other critical aspects of life, let's focus on what's happening down on earth.

There are much more fundamental forces at play for why millennials are opportunely primed beyond just one breakout election cycle or slow, patient transformation.

The thing is, it isn't just millennials who are screwed. A significant majority of Americans are screwed, record bull market be damned.

You read that correctly. In the world's largest economy (albeit, likely not for long), going through the longest bull market in its history, with unemployment at its lowest in almost two decades at 3.9 percent, as of this writing, one-third of Americans have $0 in savings, one-third have less than $1000 in savings, and fully 14 percent (45 million Americans) are living in poverty, even though they are technically employed.

The underemployment rate is much higher, at 7.5 percent. According to the Urban Institute, the average wealth of American families decreased by 30.5 percent from 2007 to 2016, while the wealth of the top 1 percent of American families has increased by 7.5 percent. There is $1.5 trillion in aggregate student debt outstanding as of June 2018. An acute shortage of affordable housing is why U.S. house prices are projected to go up twice as quickly as inflation and wages.

We could go on and on about the continuing rise in anxiety and depression among Americans, the rise in drug addiction and overdose deaths, and other signs of civilizational decay.

But with the presumption in mind that the American experiment has at least decades, if not centuries to go, let's look at what millennials can and *must* do on their own to make the best of their collective and individual situations, as well as to help others, along the way.

In my coaching practice, I've worked with hundreds of millennials, but also a sizable number of Gen Xers and even a few boomers. Inevitably, most discussions with the latter two groups defaulted to me teaching them the language and psychology of reinvention for effective career transformation, most of it being the prototypical *millennial* mindset.

What exactly, pray tell, is the *millennial mindset*? Before one client, in her early 50s, despite serious health issues in her past, phrased what I was teaching her as such, I'd never thought of it as a generational stamp.

But in fact, what I had helped her with was letting go of the essentially academic, outdated formalities of decades past, when academic degrees, prestigious institutions, and corporations with household names were essentially convenient filters for each other of perceived *quality* of job candidate, business partner, vendor, investor, adviser, or other stakeholder in a high-stakes process of creating revenue, cutting costs, and running and/or otherwise supporting an existing, high-value business.

And for decades, even centuries, this was the norm, throughout the first and second industrial revolutions. In the last 5 to 10 years, however, just as millennials have come into their own, career- and businesswise, the paradigm has shifted slowly, but significantly from that country-club world of extreme formality and prefiltering to a more flexible understanding and realization of someone's value through tangible skills learned through practice, rather than study of theory.

What I had helped my client to do was to slowly, but surely shift her mindset from *Who am I? Who cares about my story? I don't have the exact degree in X from Y or specific experience Z, plus I can't sell myself* to *I've done much more of this than I thought. I own my story. I have a great deal to contribute to others and I'm leading a movement. I know what I need and the people I need to talk to, plus how to find them and engage by adding value up front.* In short, this is the transition from a fixed to a flexible worldview, a shift from scarcity on the brain to the manifestation of plenty.

After weeks of dithering between the two seemingly irreconcilable worlds, something finally snapped. Energized and no longer hung up on formalities, she quickly began growing a massive LinkedIn network in her field (health tech), creating tens of calls and meetings with entrepreneurs and accelerator heads doing and incubating work she was strongly aligned with, getting on advisory boards, and otherwise creating and converting opportunity like she had never done or thought possible.

As a natural storyteller and writer, she had also never so much as blogged more than a few times. With some encouragement, she let go of her academic mindset in this respect, as well, and first published a blog post or two, then in Thrive Global, and only a couple short weeks later, got her first piece onto Entrepreneur.com, after taking a course from one of my own coaches who'd helped me do the same.

This was the same person who had felt stuck and inadequate and unable to make things happen just months beforehand due to negative scripts that had become acculturated into her psyche from years of (over-) education and a world that's largely changed.

To the point, this is the essence of the *Millennial mindset*, in my view. It harnesses distrust of institutions and corporations too focused on prestige and risk management to screw so many of us (and themselves, just as notably) out of opportunity and resourcefulness gained from having to move forward in life and build despite a lack of life skills or the perfect background or experience in a recession, dealing with downgrades in many elements of lifestyle and affordability, constant change and forced reinvention, high percentage school debt, plus all the other assorted systemic problems discussed previously.

When others don't give you permission to start, you have to take it yourself. In the millennial paradigm, your learned ability and speed to create and start something new, plus of course your ability to execute on opportunity once gained, become the main factors that determine your trajectory and how quickly you're able to reach your goals.

For the silent majority of millennials not on the increasingly specialized and rarified partner, offshoot, or consulting tracks of Big Law, Big Finance, Big Medicine (or Big Tech, for that matter, if you decide to FAANG (Facebook, Apple, Amazon, Netflix, Google) yourself), we must either remain content as wage slaves or learn to swim upstream and create something ourselves. As more of us get older and start families and accrue obligations in the form of mortgages, child care expenses, and the like, starting something new gets that much harder, at least timewise.

None of this is terribly novel or interesting, in that it's completely normal and expected for every generation, especially when it's never been easier to start a business quickly. That is, except for the two biggest blessings and the two biggest banes of our age—the speed and magnitude of change in all areas of our existence (as well as who initiates it, profits from it, and controls access to it) plus the unprecedented access to information we have in all areas of life.

For the first, we're not talking about change in social media trends or who controls (and misuses) our personal data, but much more about the validity of business models, the speed with which companies arise from zero to unicorn valuations and others fail spectacularly from lofty heights, as well as how those unequipped or simply unable to deal with the repercussions are forced to react to rather than anticipate change.

This comes down to simple and objective factors like one's savings balance, levels of adaptability and resilience, openness to change, and the habits to execute on the said change quickly and effectively.

If you're busy surviving from paycheck to paycheck, all the Ivy League degrees in the world won't save you from ruin when your job is eliminated or outsourced. Even with all the savviness in the world, you had no choice but to put all your proverbial eggs in one basket, since you have a family and massive loans to pay off, not to mention the dream of owning your home one day and traveling with your spouse and kids.

On the profusion of information, it is clear that access alone is no magic bullet for achieving success. If anything, too much information without context and an effective framework for absorption and application thereof leads to confusion and apathy in the vast majority of people. We know from numerous studies that a whopping 97 percent of all purchasers of online courses never actually finish them.

Too much information is simply confusing. Just Google career advice and you'll see hundreds of millions (!) of articles giving advice that's largely irrelevant, outdated, and often self-contradictory. Same goes for advice on how to start a business, pay off your student loans, find an apartment, meet your spouse, and so on and so forth.

We may be allergic to our parents' outdated advice, but at least they generally did ok flying *blind* with their parents' advice and reading books, even with dramatically fewer options than us. But then, the change they experienced in their youth and adolescence was meaningful (Woodstock, Vietnam, Nixon, Cold War), but nothing so topsy-turvy that they could speak on demand with relatives around the world, access an infinite world of information with one click, change careers essentially on a whim, start a movement with a tweet, or face ruin from a viral lie about them.

Education was cheap. A life path was generally clear early on. Real estate was reasonably priced. In short, social mobility was easier. Regulations were less pressing in all areas of life, for better or worse. Life was simpler. Privacy still existed. Time alone actually meant *alone* with one's thoughts or a book, not one's smartphone. One expected to stay in his job and profession until retirement and earned his pension to go along with social security.

None of this is to necessarily say, *woe is* us. Put plainly, our parents' generation (and to a greater degree than us, Gen X, as well), had smaller stakes to deal with through a slow and steady life progression, smaller risks to deal with in starting the life they chose (much less debt from school, cheaper housing, less upheaval from the pace of technological change).

With boomers, in particular, and to a large degree Gen X, as well, they unsurprisingly managed to accumulate much more in assets and stability, on average, than the vast majority of us in the decades-long postwar boom before the Great Recession and greatly increased inequality.

This helped them set up a life of increasing prosperity, stability, and progress which they raised us to inherit and steward to greater heights. In the simplest terms, we were raised with high—bordering on impossible—expectations for educational and professional achievement, prosperity and stability based on the sustained economic growth in the 1990s and early 2000s, which neither our parents not ourselves managed well, for the most part. Add on top of this, participation trophies and the "you can be anything you want to be" philosophy of child-raising and you get a perfect storm with a big economic downturn, the Great Recession.

Blame for this or that, which peppers the conversation on this subject, is largely beside the point. The only relevant question is, what can be done on the level of government policy and corporate social responsibility to help millennials (and Gen Zs, for that matter) to find a more solid footing in life, which is missing despite the promise (often false) of a booming economy and (overly) dynamic job market.

Millennials are long fed up with hearing damaging and misguided clichés from smug boomers and Gen Xers like "A rising tide lifts all boats," "Bootstrap your way to the top," "If you build it, they will come," and "Trickle-down economics."

There is equally fatigue about our own generation, which glorifies entrepreneurs and their bad behavior, empty boasting on social media, faking it until you make it, rags to riches stories that are too often anything but, plus other forms of signaling status and virtue, often without substance or with hypocrisy.

Status and virtue are signaled through every carefully curated choice. There are most obvious ones such as the home you live in (McMansion versus condo versus gentrifying neighborhood), car you drive (Hummer versus Prius), clothes you wear (start-up hoody or Armani suits), hair style and beard (hipster versus corporate), extending to the content you consume (indie music versus pop, Netflix versus cable, business versus entertainment podcasts, *New York Post* versus *The New York Times*, *The Wall*

Street Journal versus *The Economist*, and so on), where you get your coffee (Starbucks versus craft coffee) and beer (mass market versus craft brewery), the fact of your vote and for whom (usually a Democrat of greater or lesser progressive credentials), the quality of your experiences (travel, eating out, fancy hotels, thrill-seeking, and other bucket list items).

Then, there is also the *street cred* inherent in your personal and professional diversity of friends, colleagues, credentials, and experiences, and quite importantly, the values inherent to your workplace (cool sustainability start-up versus law firm, consulting firm, bank, or your own business).

Obsession with—or at least subconscious propensity for—constantly signaling status and virtue, plus the incessant constant comparison with others inherent in giving such signals over social media, mixed with a sense for many of us of being behind in life, added to our distrust of corporations and other institutions likewise predisposes millennials to a logical impatience with their lot.

This is why there is a common refrain among Gen X and boomer bosses about millennials jumping ship, even ghosting, to seek better titles, higher pay, and faster career and social mobility. We're always somewhere as a way station to better and better signals to send to others, as well as to ourselves and our families.

We already know we're, on average, worse off than our parents financially and, often, professionally as well. It's deeply disappointing and anxiety-causing for many of us to *know* we're behind in life and not so likely to catch up, never mind overtake our parents. We at least want to get as far as we can, as fast as we can, before everything basically goes to hell, again, maybe worse this time.

Whether or not enough millennials are in positions of power and influence quickly enough to enact change themselves before the next recession (almost surely not), before Gen Xers have their turn at depleting social security and other entitlement programs, otherwise deepening the millennial wealth gap, plus automating and outsourcing our jobs or continuing the boomer record of screwing us while blaming us for the result, it is a useful exercise to imagine the ideal state for millennials in the United States, as we increasingly grow into the stage of life and influence to enact public policy, laws and regulations, including in the workplace.

In the worst case, we'll have a useful framework with which to start once we've created the background to bring it into reality.

What is it that we millennials actually want? As covered earlier, in Chapter 1, we want mostly all the same things that all other generations before us have wanted, starting with Maslow's basics of safety, friends, and family, and continuing with achievement, self-esteem, respect of others and by others.

Plus, as eminently eligible American dreamers at work and in life, we want morality, creativity, problem solving, spontaneity, lack of prejudice, as well as —hey, why not— freedom from student debt, affordable housing, doing our life's best work in a company we love, which pays well and helps us grow quickly as people and professionals, building an amazing career and starting a successful business or two.

We want to be represented by people who *get us* and work *for* us in government, rather than by those out to disenfranchise us, insult us, rob us, and undermine our interests and values of fairness, inclusivity, more equitable economic growth, better access to inexpensive education, a more open and secure immigration policy, among other mostly progressive values. Oh yeah, that three-bedroom/two-bathhouse with a two-car garage and 2.1 kids in the suburbs would be great, too.

Is that too much to ask? Given just how much money and influence is riding on our current gerontocratic kleptocracy's protection of the crumbling status quo, wherein we're kept indebted and quiet while boomers and Gen Xers continue to rule, it most certainly seems too much to ask of our elders.

Per a favorite millennial credo, it may just be better to act and ask for an apology later than to ask for permission up front. But how exactly do we bring our tattered American dream back to life?

What is our recourse, short of voting in numbers in all available congressional, state, and presidential elections, to move the needle without waiting passively? There is something to be said for political activism, but it's taking its sweet time to materialize into actual, tangible power and change from inside our nation's democratic institutions.

The simplest and most important recourse is economics. With the already formidable spending power millennials have now, we wield the power of the consumer when it comes to demanding accountability and alignment with our values from companies whose products and services we buy. We are also beginning to realize the power of our political donations.

In turn, as more millennials start successful businesses, we wield the power to transform the way business is done, the way we treat our workers, as well as how we go through life to achieve what we see as important. This power is personal and need not wait for public policy or law to be enacted.

The second most important—yet much more difficult to attain— element of how millennials can determine their own fate is unity of purpose and mission. In a hyperpolarized democratic system splintered, confused, and made lazy (intellectually and physically) by fake news, knee-jerk name-calling, Russian trolls, Netflix and YouTube, micro-tastes for media content, microcommunities online and in real life (IRL) organized around all sorts of esoteric political, social, and other leanings, it is incredibly difficult to emerge from one's ready echo chamber of Facebook to organize active, IRL communities around a common purpose that is apolitical and instead based on the underlying problems faced by a majority of us.

But this scenario of unity is, in fact, our best chance to create change to improve our collective circumstances for the better. And this, we have no choice but to do—and quickly.

And with political gridlock here to stay along with the lack of millennial representation en masse in high political office to change things from the inside, the private sector—mainly large corporations, which wield outsized economic power, and with it, the ability to create change internally, as well as the political power to lobby for and get legislative and policy change enacted—is the best and most relevant front for millennials to engage decision makers to address the issues that matter most to them.

In so many words, given that corporations most directly answer to the laws of supply and demand, the "war for talent" is the best leverage millennials have to push for meaningful change to empower themselves to a better professional, financial, and personal trajectory.

As we've discussed previously, the most pressing issues for millennials are indebtedness; lack of quality financial planning, acumen, and execution; lack of quality career pathway planning, and management; lack of affordable housing; inability to find meaning in—and alignment with— their work and workplace and peers; lack of work–life balance or failure to integrate the two; lack of flexible work arrangements; and lack of quality business education and infrastructure to create new streams of revenue by building a successful business within or outside corporate strictures.

It's also worth noting that in our age of on-demand-everything and Netflix-and-chill coupled with millennial workaholism, soft skills centering on effective communication are ever harder to find. As such, given the strong (80 percent) correlation of millennial employee engagement when aligned with company mission, millennial social circles are increasingly built around their coworkers, to the degree that companies like WeLive (a WeWork company), Common, and others are betting big on communal housing (an extension of the college dorm room experience) as the preferred paradigm for single millennial employees.

Why should corporations care? Simply put, because they have no choice. The predominant demographic in the workplace is already—or, at least, is very soon to be—millennials, likely for the next couple of decades or more. With record job mobility in a bull market, and yet, a record number of open jobs, it's very much the candidate's market, and looks to remain that way for a long time.

Given the aforementioned millennial mores, tastes, and predicaments, which mean much more than the traditional pay-to-play paradigm for corporations in the so-called "war for talent," savvy C-suites are evolving quickly toward proactive stances and away from the reactive of the near past to attract, retain, and develop top millennial talent.

Getting talent is one thing, but getting full value from said talent means competing on multiple levels beyond just compensation. Happy employees mean happy customers. Treat employees well, and they'll be your best advocates and brand ambassadors. Treat them poorly, or even just equivocally, and they're quickly out of there, costing you 1.5 to 2 times their compensation to replace.

In an age where there is no longer distinction between personal and professional brand, *you are where you work*. And in equal measure, a successful, thriving brand is largely built on the backs of happy, engaged, and productive employees doing their life's best work for sustained and meaningful periods of time.

As such, giving one's millennial employees what they *really* want from work and life is not just a nice and lovely thing to do, but a critical necessity for a corporation's survival, not to mention for achieving a healthy bottom line, premium brand, and status of sought-after employer.

The virtuous circle of great brand, happy customers, and healthy margins and profits, plus large and growing market share, which is built on a premium and unified brand with healthy margins, lives and dies on the individual and collective engines of its employees.

And so, what is it that corporations must give millennial employees to keep them engaged, loyal, doing their life's best work, and always developing as humans and professionals?

Turns out, a lot.

As a rational actor driven by talent scarcity and the effective provider of last resort where educational institutions and legislators have lagged behind or outright failed due to lack of will, gridlock, and powerful lobbying from interest groups, the corporation must provide employee benefit support in three critical areas: remedial and continuing education, health and wellness, and ongoing financial planning and investment.

The first of these has long seen corporate involvement from the beginning, with a large proportion of top companies—especially those who prefer to train their talent in their particular work methodology—having extensive training programs as part of onboarding. Not least among this remedial and continuing education, there must be ongoing career pathway, communication, leadership, and life coaching. There is also a dramatic need for corporations to bridge the massive gap between their demand for talent with soft skills and the supply thereof in the marketplace.

It is perhaps no accident that many of these Best Places to Work For, including top consulting, tech, financial services, and consumer goods companies, have extensive remedial education for leveling up skill sets for client work and robust ongoing learning and development (L&D) programs with continuous coaching for employees.

On the health and wellness front, no high-deductible plans with Fitbits need apply. If not out of concern for real, demonstrably better health and wellness outcomes for employees, keeping up with the Joneses in tech, consulting, and other industries means companies must pony up for health, vision, dental, mental (health), and accidental (short-term and long-term disability, etc.) full or substantially full coverage for each employee and any family, in tow. And they must make available multiple options with relevant levels of coverage for each of the most common demographics. There should be options for health saving accounts (HSAs) and flexible spending accounts (FSAs) made available, along with—or at least instead of—a child care subsidy, among other highly sought benefit policies, according to a study by Deloitte.

More than just throwing in a gym subscription or fitness tracker subsidy, which don't get great utilization or provide great value for the employee in better health outcomes, on average, companies must be thoughtful about providing long-term programs proven to increase wellness (and, in turn, productivity, engagement, retention, and development) for employees. Moreover, the process should be gamified and sustainable over time to help employees get and stay fit, eat well, and maintain a healthy weight.

Lastly, but just as importantly, companies must allocate meaningful resources to 401(k) and Roth IRA matching from day 1 of employment, student loan payoff subsidies, financial planning advice, a tech budget to help them work *smart*, not just hard, and a dedicated budget for professional development such as courses, conferences, micro-degrees, and other ongoing practical training of the employee's choice.

And overall, most employees generally need assistance in becoming aware of existing benefits, as well as in how to utilize them in the best way for them and their families.

If all of this seems a tall order, it may well be, at least for now, especially if we look through the quaint lenses of yesteryear's talent wars waged with bonuses and trophies.

But rules change. Appetites and sensibilities change. And no company is immune to the vagaries of the talent marketplace.

The corporations that survive and thrive in the coming two to three decades despite—or perhaps because of—the relentless pace of tech and business model innovation in our age will not be those that follow talent trends retroactively, but rather those that create a superior employee experience for their millennials and, increasingly, older executives.

In short, the proverbial train has left the station.

Summary

Millennial Voices—how do we see ourselves and what is unique to us and what isn't? Who are the millennials that *speak for us*? How accurate is that representation? How to empower millennials to come into their own, have their voice heard, contribute the greatest value to those they work for, sell to, buy from, invest in, their investors, advisers, and so on?

CHAPTER 4

Millennial Vices

It has been my experience that folks who have no vices have very few virtues.

—Abraham Lincoln

Boomers and Gen Xers love to wax self-righteous about supposed millennial *vices*, code for *these millennials have watered down our standards and everything's going to hell because of it*, and they see the world a different way from us, their parents and older siblings. Some millennials have even disowned themselves publicly from the rest of us lost souls.

We've covered quite a few of the *vices* that are really just false stereotypes of millennials and inaccurate as to our supposed differences from older generations at the same stage in life, earlier, in Chapter 1.

But surely, we *are* different from the other generations, and not always for the better, right? Surely, there can't be smoke without a fire . . . can there be?

Inevitably, the answer is both yes and no, with some surprising twists.

First, when it comes to actual vice, millennials are lagging behind previous generations on several big fronts. They're having less sex than any generation in 60 years, drinking less beer (albeit more wine and spirits), taking fewer hard drugs (or at least hiding it better), committing fewer crimes than previous generations did at this stage, and are financially savvier (if less well off) than previous generations, on average. Even the perception of most millennials as casual weed smokers is false possibly due to increasing legalization and regulation, with baby boomers still well ahead of millennials in cannabis consumption.

By several measures, including preference for life insurance at the same or higher level as other benefits, as well as a smaller likelihood of starting a business on their own than previous generations, millennials are the most risk-averse generation since the Great Depression.

Maybe it's due to the higher average education level. Some posit five factors as mostly responsible for why we're so sober and serious: selfie obsession, academic pressures, depression and anxiety, technology addiction, and cocooning.

No, we can't all make it to Burning Man every year, so we have to huddle around the one in a thousand who actually did and listen to their stories of wild drug use, sex, costumes, and tech.

Regarding healthy eating and lifestyle, the jury is still out. On the one hand, there is worrying evidence of millennials eating out significantly more than other generations, binge-watching Netflix, ordering everything on demand to the home, and not having enough support in life and career to focus meaningfully on healthy eating. One thing is for sure, everything tastes better with Sriracha, but the rising rate of bowel cancer among millennials means not all is well with our diet and lifestyle.

On the other hand, we have unprecedented access to medical and nutritional knowledge and consult with relevant health professionals at a higher frequency, and are more likely to consume superfoods like kale, chia seeds, and cayenne pepper. The potential for healthy aging is greater for millennials than any other generation due to awareness, social pressure, and the risks to image and employment associated with bad health. Actually living up to the lifestyle standards necessary to achieve healthy aging is another matter. The takeaway is that at least, we eat healthy-ish, sort-of.

When it comes to the workplace, career, and business the data about millennial work *vices* is more complex. First, we know that millennials are the most educated generation of all time, especially millennial women.

Regarding the workplace, some sources conclude that millennials are actually workaholics while maintaining the same level of work ethic as previous generations, even as others insist that millennials have a worse work ethic than Gen Xers and boomers at the same stage. A meta-study of 77 others shows no difference between the generations. At the same time, millennials experience and dish out vacation shaming and work martyrdom more than other generations.

On the front of constant connectedness, millennials are actually slightly behind their Gen X colleagues and bosses, who are just as tech savvy as millennials; use social media more, on average, every day; and also happen to occupy the majority of the senior leadership positions in companies as of this writing.

Much has been made of millennial impatience and overambition, but as discussed in Chapter 1, the data doesn't support this conclusion. Once more, the average job tenure of millennials today is right on par with—or even higher than—that of previous generations at the same career stage.

So do millennials actually have their proverbial stuff together, despite all the hype about us? Shockingly for those who dispense and buy the hype, the answer is yes, on average, for many critical measures, including health, morals, work ethic, savviness in tech and finances, among others. There may even, sort of, be a case to make for millennials as a cohort as a tad too sober and serious.

But let's not get carried away. The mix between selfie + tech obsession, academic and professional pressure, and cocooning on the one hand and high student debt load, risk aversion, and the large and widening wealth gap, on the other hand, is a toxic and heavy one.

Little surprise, then, that millennials tend to have a high—and rising—risk of depression and anxiety and other mental health issues. Self-medication is also rampant, not least through the widespread use of cannabis and alcohol.

Things may look great on social media, but most of us are just making the best we can of life, despite the latent effects of being screwed.

When we look more closely into the entrepreneur phenomenon among millennials, several themes quickly arise that give us a glimpse into the collective millennial psyche.

First, millennials are rampant in hero worshipping entrepreneurs, despite the last spate of scandals in Silicon Valley. Elon Musk, Mark Zuckerberg, Sergey Brin, Steve Jobs, Richard Branson, Marc Benioff, and others come to mind.

On the one hand, this sets up unrealistic and dangerous illusions of riches at the end of tech Initial Public Offering (IPO) or funding round rainbows. On the other, it provides a hopeful window from the window-less cubicle of corporate misery, benefit-less gig economy, the staggering weight of student debt, high rate of start-up failure, and the ability of the tech oligopoly to crush nascent innovation or acqui-hire it.

By and large, we millennials have our own Kool-Aid that we mix daily for an online audience and that we likewise eat up from others. The sheer volume and frequency with which we consume and share private content online—often with perfect strangers, settings permitting—on social media and elsewhere means we are curating our lives for the benefit of friends, family, and strangers, expecting judgment and comparison from others and engaging in it ourselves, in return.

In our social media culture, we easily find possibly millions of photos posted monthly by millennial *entrepreneurs* on FB, Instagram, and elsewhere in front of rented luxury cars or other false status symbols, acting out the *fake it 'til you make it* ethos.

The simple truth is that the vast majority of them are either dead broke and just plainly faking it, whereas the successful few are often (albeit not always) made such by serious financial support from parents. "The Myth of the Self-Made Millennial" like Kylie Jenner is an old one, by this point.

And millennials know the game, because when they're not playing it themselves, they're trolling or hating on other players—or calling them on their bullsh*t.

The con extends to a daily flood of posts (my own FB news feed alone is a marvel) by entrepreneurs spouting *easy* formulas to success and just-so stories of five- and six-figure months (even days) in their business, plus generalized advice to uplift and coax others into purchasing their products, clicking, liking, and sharing their lead magnet, and so on. Some have recently found FB and LinkedIn algorithmic gold for engagement by baring their soul and showing their failures on the way to those six-figure months.

In a precious few cases, entrepreneurs really get *raw* in telling the full extent of their failures, wanderings, dead ends, personal and professional problems on the way to some modest success. But by and large, in one online entrepreneur community after next, there is a toxic mix of optimism about potential outcomes, cynicism about the filth behind the veneer of success, plus a never-ending race to produce and share content on every platform and in every form possible to create and convert leads.

The numbers from academic studies on the subject bear out the anecdotes. While popular perception has it that millennials are all either actual or aspiring entrepreneurs, the facts show a mixed and quite a different picture. A significantly smaller percentage of millennials are actually *self-employed*—a proxy measure of entrepreneurship—than of Gen Xers or boomers, although this percentage is set to rise dramatically by 2020. In fact, according to the same survey, a full 42 percent of the expected influx of self-employed workers will come from the millennial group, although this may simply be the case due to age, life stage, and the lack of meaning-ful family and financial obligations when becoming self-employed.

Even so, when we dig past the optimistic tone, the numbers show that millennials are not only less entrepreneurial in practice, but also fail more in their actual entrepreneurship. In short, everyone wants to be a success story and overestimates their chances of success on the basis of social media, but when push comes to shove, most just can't hack it. And this is despite ample evidence to show it's never been easier to start a business at any point in history.

Success in business clearly takes much more than just starting one. Taking risks isn't the only measure that leads to success. The main factors are resilience and runway—resilience to see the business to success and enough runway to prove product–market fit and actually sell a product or service enough to sustain a minimum viable lifestyle (MVL).

The simplest reason why the vast majority of millennials fail to start—or fail to succeed in—their own business is lack of follow-through and grit to see a business succeed. Behind this is the inability to take sustained risks due to massive student debt. We may be dependent on staying in a corporate job to have benefits and maintain financial goals.

Interestingly enough, the average number of companies started per millennial (7.7) is significantly higher than for other generations, al-though this number appears to be quite skewed by a small number of nonfirst-generation serial entrepreneurs starting a string of businesses, rather than a large number of first-time entrepreneurs starting their first (at 22 percent, well below the almost 50 percent of boomers who started one). Moreover, younger millennials seem to be more amenable to the risk of starting their own companies than older millennials, who were more affected in their early career by the Great Recession.

In short, for all the millennial hype and reverence for entrepreneur-ship, there are many fewer of us actually jumping into the deep end of entrepreneurship and a yet much smaller proportion of us are actually successful in starting and building businesses. For all the hundreds of hyped-up, self-selected stories of successful tech and other entrepreneurs pushed by PR and media folks that we hear, there are hundreds of thousands of failures yearly.

And as much as most aspiring entrepreneurs seek the *freedom* of starting one's own business, along with the rarified riches of large VC rounds or being able to make one's own hours while partying with celebrities, the harsh truth is that the vast majority of entrepreneurs just can't hack it in business, for a variety of reasons, or otherwise just become slaves to their *own* business, rather than someone else's.

In the end, those who tend to *make it* are both dogged and tend to be supported by investment and/or guidance from a network of successful entrepreneurs (their parents, schoolmates, etc.), have little or no school debt, and are otherwise much better versed and supported in their entrepreneurial endeavors than the rest of us (see https://www.vox.com/first-person/2017/1/17/14263282/startup-founder-privilege).

It looks like there's no avocado toast in hipster Brooklyn without a trust fund to pay for it. LOLZ, #KiddingNotKidding. But more on that later.

To sum up, if we millennials are guilty of any *vice*, it's hopeful optimism without follow through, day dreaming without *paying our dues*, wanting more than we're given by circumstances without accepting our fate, wanting our gluten-free cake and eating it too.

But this *vice* is really just nothing more than the same, completely normal self-interest all young people have had in the past, with no unreasonable expectation of achieving the American Dream other than that the timing and conditions are more difficult for us than for the two generations ahead of us in life.

If we are guilty of wanting the American Dream, we can hardly be blamed for it. If we're hopeless optimists about our own potential and cynical about those demonizing it, then we're just like all the young people who came before us.

Summary

Millennial Vices—where is criticism deserved and what are the areas for improvement in perception and execution?

CHAPTER 5

Psychology/Mindset

There is no simple way to color every member of a generation with broad strokes, especially around psychology and mindset. To get the closest we can to identifying patterns thereof, we can look at defining historical events, socioeconomic conditions, prevalent technology, pop culture, plus any mass movements and their collective and individual impact on expectations and outcomes.

For historical events, the vast majority of millennials lived consciously through 9/11, the wars in Iraq and Afghanistan, the Great Recession, George W.'s, Obama's and Trump's first elections, al-Qaeda's terrorist outrages, the Columbine shooting, Hurricane Katrina, the launch of Facebook, Snowden's revelations, among other more localized events like natural disasters (earthquakes, floods, tornadoes, hurricanes).

Older millennials will also remember the end of the Cold War in 1991, the Lewinsky scandal, the first World Trade Center bombing, the O.J. Simpson Trial, Oklahoma City bombing, among others.

In socioeconomic terms, we went from a time of increasing prosperity mostly across the board (much of the Clinton years) when most of us were between fetal and high schoolers to a tech bust, then 5 to 6 years of recovery and job growth until the Great Recession, with increases in education costs far outpacing inflation and wage growth, ever-rising student debt, rising real estate costs, and an otherwise overheating economy with a widening wealth and wage gap. On the vice prevention side, many of us went through Drug Abuse Resistance Education (DARE) and some also through abstinence-only Sex Ed., down South.

Those older millennials (xennials, they've been called) who were *lucky* enough to start their careers before the Great Recession got in at least a few years of meaningful wage growth and career progression as a push forward, whereas those who were in school or otherwise just starting their careers experienced a massive setback in the form of unemployment, stunted wage growth, not to mention massive workforce reductions and business model shifts as in law and finance, resulting in increased outsourcing, automation, and elimination of many types of jobs forever.

On the technology front, within a few years, we went from rarely ever seeing cell phones to their ubiquity, as well as the spread and mass adoption of laptops, ICQ and AOL Instant Messenger, then social media including Friendster, MySpace, and most importantly, Facebook, Twitter, and LinkedIn. The rise of the smartphone has brought an *always-on* mentality both from employers, family, and ourselves, making loneliness easier and more prevalent, as well as accelerating a lack of social cohesion, given an easy fallback to limitless content consumption.

More than just tethering us 24/7 to our work, news feeds, and cat videos, one of the most amazing effects of technology in the last 10 years has been the explosion of crowdsourcing, crowdfunding, and other crowd-driven decision making.

Rather than trust Yelp or another platform with strangers' biased—or outright made-up—reviews, many millennials reflexively crowdsource their personal social networks for all sorts of decisions, like which pediatrician to visit in Chicago, where to get a plumber in Reno the best cupcake in Barcelona, which destinations to visit in a certain country, and what cryptocurrency or cannabis business to invest in.

The Securities and Exchange Commission (SEC)'s regulatory loosening that's enabled and empowered crowdfunding for the masses has led to an explosion of platforms and start-ups preselling everything from revolutionary juicers to newfangled watches and software on Kickstarter, IndieGogo, and what seems like hundreds of clones.

On other tech fronts, YouTube has made video the most consistently engaging content by time spent per session, while Netflix not only made retail video stores obsolete, but also invested massively into developing original shows and film, creating a gold rush by Amazon, Hulu, HBO, and finally Disney and others to democratize content creation and consumption away from control by the large film studios and TV network, also helping to unbundle cable and cut the cord, once and for all. Facebook's

Live and its spirit on LinkedIn and elsewhere have made broadcasting live video—and content creation, in general—easy as pie.

The low and decreasing cost of producing high-quality video, audio, print, and digital content has led to an explosion of content creation across all media, both leading to an endless flood of content created, posted, and shared every single day and making the value of each piece of content essentially zero. As mentioned earlier, a whopping 97 percent of all purchasers of online courses never actually finish them.

But just as importantly, the profusion of content has created loyal tribes of listeners, readers, customers, and in turn, employees out of groups of highly engaged and loyal fans for podcasts, shows, articles, books, and brands, overall.

Facebook has made comparing oneself to friends and others in the network a staple of everyday living during all hours, leading to further isolation, anxiety, and depression, despite a demonstrable bias by users to curate their posts toward unrealistically happy images of themselves on vacation, eating, hanging out with friends and the like.

Instagram has further accelerated this unrealistic image making and made it the standard way to broadcast status. As a result, adults and children alike engage in comparing themselves to others in every form of social media as a daily, often hourly exercise.

Twitter has made broadcasting short messages to a mass audience easy as a click, helping start revolutions in the Arab world, flash mobs, and tweet storms. This has given many armchair commentators a false sense of aggrandizement, not least our president. Yet more importantly, the speed, ease of use, ubiquity, and easy manipulation of social media has, unsurprisingly, led to the profusion of not just images and narratives of *fake it 'til you make it*, but the creation and spread of *fake news* with the help of rogue state and nonstate actors like Russia, China, North Korea, and other dictatorships (see https://www.clingendael.org/sites/default/files/2018-05/Report_Hybrid_Conflict.pdf).

The downfall of science and medicine as the last frontiers of truth has resulted from the increasing politicization of science, shrinking research budget allocations, and a rocketing rate of research article retractions in top magazines. No wonder most people resort to Dr. Google before making their appointment.

More disturbingly, the rise of *deep fakes* is making it downright impossible to tell the truth from *truthiness*. And as icing on the cake, the president's personal lawyer (Rudy Giuliani) says on national television that "truth is not truth."

On the more buttoned-up, professional side, LinkedIn has standardized the way we display ourselves professionally to the outside world, often becoming the first entry in a Google search for our names. This has, nevertheless, failed to prevent the conflation of personal and professional brand and the adjustment of both to more cleanly fit with the other, in mind and in deed, at work.

Skype, WhatsApp, Viber, and most of all, FaceTime have made free, instantaneous communication possible with anyone, anywhere in the world, giving both comfort and joy to family far away and accessibility to far-flung people, but also accelerating the *always-on* and *always-available* sensibilities.

Snapchat has made it easy for anyone to share anything vapid, racy, or stupid with friends with minimal risk to outside exposure—and Google indexing. That is, with the exception of Snapchat's own data collection.

This progression of social media tech has taken us from guarding our privacy to having none, then to feeling social pressure to share (and curate) our public online image all the time, from being mostly IRL (in real life) to mostly online, from having illusions of privacy from government monitoring and data collection to expecting all communications at all times to be within the government's and tech's purview.; All promises to the contrary are no longer being taken seriously.

One important benefit created by social media aside from speed and ease of communication is that it's taken away the need for much time or overhead costs to start a business by allowing leverage of our social networks quickly to sell anything, needing only a smartphone and a PayPal link to bring in revenue.

The dark side of social media and related tech has been the anonymity that unchains trolls to threaten anyone, anywhere with exposing their address, private photos, ill-advised comments, or other damaging material. Much of this is done by trolls and cyberbullies with few, if any, repercussions (some states have enacted—or are in the process of enacting—laws to counteract this) (see https://

www.businessinsider.com/why-now-is-the-best-time-to-start-a-company-2014-10; https://www.forbes.com/sites/johnrampton/2015/04/09/10-tips-to-dealing-with-trolls).

The other negative effects of social media include addiction, isolation, lack of social development for kids and adults, unrealistic images of *success* from entrepreneurs and peers, as well as the complete loss of privacy and inability to bury or timely delete ill-advised tweets and FB posts that harm reputation, often very quickly and irreparably (see http://www.bbc.com/future/story/20180104-is-social-media-bad-for-you-the-evidence-and-the-unknowns; https://www.forbes.com/sites/alicegwalton/2017/06/30/a-run-down-of-social-medias-effects-on-our-mental-health).

Loss of privacy through authorized and unauthorized user data access has exacerbated and normalized the effects and extent of hacking, customized ads trailing you everywhere, fake news targeting by state and nonstate actors to influence elections and commit fraud and theft, the creation of an echo chamber in our online (and, in turn, real) life, further splitting us along the tribal lines according to signals of status and virtue.

One other tech trend that has seeped into our daily routine is the on-demand delivery of food (Instacart, AmazonFresh, UberEats, and others), media (Amazon, Netflix, Hulu, HBO, many others), consumer goods (Amazon, Alibaba), money (PayPal, Venmo, many others), transportation (Uber/Lyft and clones, Car2Go, Maven, Citi Bike, Bird, Lime, etc.), and a massive variety of services and information (TaskRabbit, Pager, Fiverr and Upwork, Trulia/Zillow, tutoring, coaching, tailoring, interior design, etc.), plus seemingly everything else.

Technology around instant communication, sharing, and collaboration (Slack, Trello, Skype, Zoom, and many others) has made work more flexible and often just as easily done remotely. The way we learn, even if it still usually starts with Google and Wikipedia, is often undertaken without thought of accreditation or grades, through MOOCs and all sorts of gamified micro-learning and celebration of small wins. On-demand and sharing economy business models have helped millions create side hustles and profitable businesses from work outsourced anywhere around the world with the talent and wage arbitrage to benefit all involved.

Overall, even as tech innovation has leveled off in the last few years due to consolidation and an oligopoly by FAANG in the tech industry, the speed of change in our lives thanks to evolving technology has continued increasing. The next wave is already here, with the internet of things (IoT), artificial intelligence (AI), machine learning, and blockchain being integrated into every corner of our personal and business lives. The jury is still out as to the extent of job automation and loss to expect in the coming years, as well as the extent of the benefit to our Gross Domestic Product (GDP), to say nothing of the massive potential for everything from more accurate diagnoses of disease to better business decisions, and so on.

The speed of change, while exhilarating, is the source of great uncertainty and anxiety for millennials and all other adults equally, in the absence of protections from uber-intelligent robots set to take over our lives, a universal living wage to buttress against massive job automation, and other safeguards for those not owning or otherwise in control of the technologies integral to our personal and professional lives.

Standing on one foot, this progression has taken millennials from the middle or end of childhood innocence to the constant specter, then expectation of terrorism, sex scandals, online shaming, school shootings, small and shrinking attention span, lack of civility in public discourse, massive debt, job losses and diminished earning potential, climate-related natural disasters, plus major life events (starting a family, getting better jobs, buying a home, starting a business) later than expected in life (if ever) and at a more modest level than we were brought up to expect. Cry me a river or not, these formative experiences have clearly left their mark.

In short, the most coddled generation brought up on promises of gold at the end of rainbows suddenly had its bubble burst through a series of awful, large-scale events out of its control, and has had to react with as much pragmatic optimism as possible to better its lot. That is to say, even while looking cynically at the work, promises, privilege, and guidance of older generations, who helped construct or bring about those very socio-economic and world-historical circumstances like war, rising inequality, stagnant wages, unemployment, and climate change.

Imagine going from a sheltered suburban childhood with little care in the world except looking cool in school and getting good grades while playing sports for fun to leaving college 4 years later with $25K in debt to start a job in a field you've been groomed for your entire life, only to lose your job in the recession, then do grad school and rack up another

$200K in loans, graduate into a field with few jobs, then have to *wing it* in life by getting temp jobs, surviving between projects, starting a family, living in far-from-affordable housing, always living paycheck to paycheck while giving away essentially all of it for housing, food, expenses, and loan repayment. Imagine making bad decisions because of missing financial savvy on top of anxiety and depression from not yet knowing your purpose and meaning in life due to *circumstances*.

This is what makes it hard for so many millennials—and Americans of all generations, in general—to support a family, save up to buy a home, never mind for their children's education, savings, travel, and so on.

On a lighter note, millennials have made do as best they can, even quite well on some accounts. On the food front, for instance, the organic/artisanal, local/slow, world fusion food movement has taken off among millennials, driven by Whole Foods, Trader Joe's, and local competitors, as well as farmers' markets and food trucks as a lower-risk alternative to restaurants.

At the same time, craft coffee, craft beer, and even previously "exotic" condiments have become increasingly popular with the rise of urban hipster culture. The latter stands for little of anything concrete except contrarianism to established orthodoxies, small comforts in life, casual dress and speech, flexibility in work and family arrangements, being non-judgmental except of those prejudged as *personae non grata*, especially anyone accused of clinging to guns, religion, and other *red state* elements of worldview.

As for pop culture, millennials have witnessed a transition from the grunge of the early 1990s to rap & R&B on MTV and VH1; the scourge of reality TV; an explosion of unbundled and easily shared content of all sorts; an Internet broken periodically by Kim Kardashian's behind, Trump's tweets, and arguments about dress colors—plus a fractured media landscape, culture wars played out along well-established lines, and a love–hate relationship with the glamour and screwups of tech moguls.

In the workplace, millennials are more open (some would say, more shameless) than previous generations in asking of their potential employers a redeeming social mission (not just prestige) that reflects well on their own personal/professional brand (the two have no practical distinction, any longer), a diverse and inclusive workforce, an environment where they receive regular feedback from their manager, an HR framework that not only pays them fairly and takes care of their health and finances, but also utilizes more of their talents and surrounds them with people they respect and who respect them.

And perhaps more than anything else, millennials are looking for managers who display constructive empathy (if not always radical transparency), listen with an ear to understand—not micromanage—and focus on helping the employee as a human and professional develop and become the best version of him- or herself. The boss and company that care keep top talent around longer, in part because they're so rare in a corporate world obsessed with the bottom line, innovation—anything other than creating a culture of care at work.

They also greatly value a culture that celebrates small wins, gives them flexible (in particular, remote) work arrangements and some freedom to pursue side projects, as well as gives them both open and anonymous means to communicate with management the things they like and dislike, so they can be quickly fixed and/or improved. Millennials are keen on working smart, not just hard, which means having a dedicated budget for the latest tech and productivity tools, as well as a concerted learning and development (L&D) framework that helps them build their own brand through contributed thought leadership, speaking, and teaching other team members and industry colleagues.

A *no asshole* rule is very popular in VC-backed tech start-ups, including The Muse, where the policy has repeatedly passed muster in my interactions with employees. In short, working with people you get along with, learn from, and respect mutually is no longer a luxury, but a requirement, given millennials' workaholism and impatience with moving up quickly to bigger and better things.

In all, there is generally growing awareness in companies of multiple career options for employees and highly varied trajectories and greater ownership of employees' journeys and life stories. This may be due to the growth of a therapy culture and/or the emergence of tens of thousands of coaches and consultants easily available on demand for every kind of career, life, and business in the last decade.

Socially, millennials have experienced a time of greater urbanization (more young people moving to or working in urban areas) and gentrification (the conversion of urban downtowns and ho-hum suburbs into tony hipster havens), as well as diversity (more immigrants from all parts of the world as a percent of the U.S. population, a rising proportion of minorities and women in the workplace, politics, and other areas of life), inclusiveness (gay marriage and nonbinary gender identity recognition), and the attendant legal protections therefor.

Save for high-growth tech start-ups run by bros now in deep water for lack of diversity and inclusion (D&I; see Uber and a long line of others), millennials for the most part expect and value the presence of and collaboration with people of different backgrounds and worldviews. Perhaps due to the lingering effects of the Great Recession, millennials are both less mobile and more rooted than previous generations.

Religiously, millennials tend to be less religiously observant, even if they seek spirituality in all sorts of nonreligious pursuits to make up for the void of existential structure and explanation. The institution of marriage has undergone an evolution with millennials. The stigma of living together without being married, even with kids, is long gone. Many millennials choose not to marry or at least to marry later, when they are better situated financially and professionally. As such, it's interesting to note that millennials are the driving force behind an 18 percent drop in the divorce rate between 2008 and 2016. Even so, marriage is less common and largely an event earned, rather than arranged with much less regard for the couple's life circumstances, as in the past.

On the subject of managing expectations, a bevy of social apps ranging from Tinder and Bumble to Shapr and a thousand others have spurred an expectation of on-demand transactional encounters by choice, making unfocused networking unnecessary and lower in quality, as well as spurring curated IRL events (dinners, business speed dating, etc.) prearranged for fit and quality and focused on a clear theme.

On the social front, especially for urban millennials, there has never been a more exciting time in history to assume whatever identity they wish, in any forum they wish; to create content; as part of a tribe online and/or IRL, anywhere around the world, around any cause, product, brand, service— or for no reason at all—for free or next to nothing.

On the flip side. There has also never been a more anxiety-ridden time, given the easily searchable digital record one leaves online, ridden with youthful indiscretions and other *inconvenient* truths of growing up before knowing all the rigid and subtle rules of corporate America. There is now, more than ever, a myriad ways in which self-selection, unconscious bias, and purposeful discrimination still very much affect everything, including hiring, credit, housing, academic admission, as well as all sorts of basic, social, and financial decisions.

We may not be quite at the level of China's dystopic social credit system, but AI, machine learning, and the increasing migration of every area of life to the blockchain will go only further to eliminate the potential for human error and fraud, even while potentially institutionalizing some form of bias into every decision critical to accessing opportunity.

Rather than solely being a cause for conscious or unconscious bias or discrimination by employers or prospective mates, affiliation with any particular group or identity (within legal and mainstream ethical boundaries) can instead mean a wealth of opportunity in business, career, or personal life. But for the vast majority of those millennials who must compete for a job, housing, credit, funding, and other milestones critical for adult existence, family, and professional life, the corpus of data available about them is a source of constant anxiety and uncertainty.

Any social media post not sufficiently anodyne, any formal or informal litmus test failed through a racy photo or offhand retweet, article written for the *wrong* audience or cause supported—or even just a photo that's cause for damnation by association—can instantly derail a career, make one lose a job, lead to a boycotted and dead business, denied membership to professional associations, not to mention social ostracism.

Sensitivity—and obedience—to an informal and ever-shifting *code* of conduct and presentation of self in public and professional fora is a delicate and increasingly difficult dance for millennials to manage, since they no longer have the folly of youth to excuse behavior adjudged unacceptable nor have the tangible power in politics or corporations to change policy, enact law, or otherwise shape public discourse meaningfully.

Being under a constant microscope from all sides—when one has no *f*ck-you money* or political power and when one is dependent on the very people in power who demonize your entire generation for a living—has a tremendous chilling effect on social and political activism that's not as easy as protesting Trump's policies or climate change, conservative dogma, or any of the other "easy" pet liberal causes and issues.

Hence, it isn't difficult to understand why millions of students and young adults aren't protesting in Washington against draconian student debt policies, lack of affordable housing, police brutality, or much any other issue of unique generational import.

Millennials are, on the one hand, the most educated and coddled generation raised on the promise of an outsized influence in an ever-growing globalist economy and superior world order based on classical liberal values; on the other hand, they are a generation screwed by the economy, older generations' selfish and wrongheaded decision making and institutions we don't trust, runaway technological change and economic shifts favoring aging kleptocrats and the ultra-wealthy, as well as a surveillance state in bed with a tech oligopoly.

The simple truth remains that we as a generation have much more to win from continued cooperation in a globalist democracy based on classical liberal values and the skewed market economy run by aging kleptocrats and older elites. That is, as long as they maintain the promise of giving us the opportunity of moving up slowly, but surely, in our personal and professional lives, than from any alternative of our creation or others' imposition. In short, the overwhelming majority of us feel we're better off trying to change the political and economic system slowly from the inside, rather than calling and protesting for wholesale change.

If and when this calculus changes, then it will be a different conversation, but for now, our current world order is all we know as Americans (except those of us hyphenated Americans brought up under totalitarian regimes like Soviet Russia, communist China, and others).

And more than anything, millennials know that any semblance of a safety net in the form of social security and other *entitlements* like unemployment benefits and Medicare is small, insufficient, and shrinking by design thanks to conservatives in power (themselves quite wealthy, on average), leaving us with little to no room for error in *getting it right* with our careers, finances, and lives, in general.

We've often got nobody but ourselves to rely on, because our parents and extended family are also just barely making it in life, due to stagnant wages, longer life, and the lingering effects of investment loss in the

Great Recession. The proof for this is the low and shrinking rate of social mobility.

This is the main—and simplest—reason for why millennials tend to be risk averse, less entrepreneurial and mobile, for why we are fond of the sharing economy and other ways to save money and pool resources for better mutual outcome.

We haven't necessarily given up on the American Dream of a family with 2.1 kids, a steady job, a three-bedroom house in the suburbs with a two-car garage. We're just much more sober eyed about what it will take to actually reach those goals. But even if it's taken longer than expected, many of us are well on the way.

On a separate—and mixed—note for democracy, the surge of diverse and inclusive voices and fora and policies has led to checked privilege, white guilt, and the rightful outing of sexual harassers and predators in positions of power, while empowering (at least in theory) for diverse and inclusive voices. Concrete change in boardrooms and halls of political power has been slower than the rhetoric would suggest, but is picking up steam. This development has been a big blow for the traditional power base of conservative white males, which, judging by the presidential representative thereof, is embattled.

Notably, the culture wars on steroids between conservatives and liberals in the United States have effectively silenced centrists of all stripes and laid all sorts of hidden mines in our democratic discourse around racism, genderism, *acceptable* and *unacceptable* opinions in the field of discourse, effectively reducing it to either anodyne or dog-whistle talking points and tropes broadcast on Twitter for the benefit of *the supportive base* by both sides, creating an insulated echo chamber that's potentially one market crash or police-caused death away from social unrest and outright violence.

The two sides have simply never been more trigger-happy and ready to destroy the *other*, no longer even feigning anything like a common interest in the health of our democracy or republic, rather obsessed with *getting even* and naked self-interest. The fringes from both sides have gone mainstream and the incumbent *adults* in the room (boomers and Gen Xers beholden to principle or at least corporate lobbying interests) are getting voted out of office, tarred and feathered in the media. Time will tell if it's a revolution or jumping the shark.

And so, millennials and others have on paper never been freer to express their opinions on gender, race, identity, or any other field of inquiry, but only insofar as their opinions must hew closely to narrow prevailing orthodoxies in the halls of power, the academe, and corporate boardrooms. One wrong word, opinion, statement, photo can lead instantly to demonization, death threats, loss of career, and downstream effects for oneself and one's family. Choosing one's words carefully is a hallmark of modern American existence in an era of political correctness gone amok.

We have never been closer together through technology, yet we've never been further apart from each other due to lack of common purpose, fractionated into social, political, culinary, sartorial, generational, ethical, and ethnic micro-groups, connected by little more than institutions we distrust, laws and regulations that favor the wealthy and privileged.

We live in times that have never been better by standards of life, health, and average income, yet we're so anxious and depressed that we seek escape any way we can.

Our entire conscious lives, we've been sold a bill of goods about an American Dream that hasn't quite materialized for too many of us, or at least nowhere near as quickly. We're no longer drinking the Kool-Aid, but we're also not ready to puncture the bubble and demand change through sustained activism, either. Too self-absorbed, self-interested, and unsure of where the world is going, most of us are in a holding pattern, waiting for Godot or otherwise affecting change on a smaller, local level, for now.

We maintain the illusion of eternal progress by sticking to outdated, misleading measures of health (life expectancy) and wealth (GDP per capita, real estate prices), hoping and praying that the structural problems in our society and economy don't come to a head—or at least don't blow up in our faces—too soon or too abruptly.

While this chapter is nominally about millennials in America, the majority of elements of mindset and psychology described herein are equally applicable for large proportions of Gen Xers, boomers, and Gen Zers, since we are all largely in the same boat with similar pursuits, wants and needs, technology we use, and political, societal, and economic constraints on our opportunity, success, and livelihoods. The only difference is that some of us are later or earlier in the journey, with different elements of background we're born with, levels of education, cyclical economic and social circumstances, opportunities, and the ability to convert opportunities into success.

America has always been based on exceptionalism and building a better system for future generations, as much as it was built on reinvention of self. While the sense of exceptionalism has come and largely gone in our time, the reinvention part is as relevant as ever in an era of massive technological and economic change.

Only time will tell whether those institutions we distrust and the self-interested gerontocrats who run them and bash us at will save the American experiment again when the next recession, bubble, spasm of social unrest, and partisan culture wars erupt when the fig leaf of nominal common interest in preserving our republic is ripped off.

It also remains to be seen just when—not if—millennials fully assert themselves as a political and economic force at that time, demanding meaningful change as a group like the boomers did in the late 1960s and early 1970s, no longer remaining silent bystanders who flock to economic, social, and political safety.

We may be a bit late in the game compared with our boomer parents at our age, but as every generation has in the past, we will continue to have our defining moments. With America still humming along and with plenty of growth left and fuel being plentiful, there is yet cause for optimism, even with hyper-partisan politics and totalitarian regimes striking at our credibility and infrastructure from afar.

***

Summary

Psychology/Mindset—how we think, what is unique (digital natives, lack of patience), what is same as for other generations before us going through this stage of their lives; discussion of our anxiety and decreasing religiosity, lack of rootedness and yet lesser mobility than past generations

CHAPTER 6

Language

THIS. LOLZ. Literally #TheBestEver.

In our still relatively short, millennial lifetimes, the world has changed dramatically on the fronts of technology, security, geopolitics, education, language, and psychology, altering everything from how we interact with the world, how we process information, make decisions, plan and execute, work, play, travel, and create and consume content.

If knowledge is power, as we've been told repeatedly since childhood, then language—both the one we speak in our own minds and the one we use to communicate—is the means of projecting (or ceding) that power.

The language we use to interact with others and the world at large, as the first front where change is most easily apparent, has also undergone a dramatic shift.

For instance, communicating with others has evolved from mostly one-on-one with occasional phone conversations and some snail mail and e-mail to mostly tech based (e-mail, text, FaceTime/Skype, Facebook Messenger, WhatsApp, Twitter, Snapchat, Slack, Instagram, and so on) and less one-on-one.

The sheer volume of messages, texts, posts, and e-mails we send and receive every single day has continued to grow exponentially over the last few years (see https://www.forbes.com/sites/bernardmarr/2018/05/21/how-much-data-do-we-create-every-day-the-mind-blowing-stats-everyone-should-read/#22db1b9260ba; https://www.eetimes.com/author.asp?section_id=36&doc_id=1330462). As with ever faster Wi-Fi and site loading times, better cellular coverage, faster and more accurate search capability, our expectation of prompt answers from others to our messages has also increased, creating an increasingly transactional nature to our conversations, with less and less patience allotted with every faster and more capable smartphone, laptop, tablet, and other hardware and software further raising the stakes.

While the benefits of dispensing with formalities and of faster, more direct, and more frequent communication are generally clear for business, they have led to a spike in the average time spent on the phone and computer by young and old, alike—meaning (by inference) less time and (by extension) less quality time spent one-one-one with family, friends, and colleagues.

Technology has reinforced bad habits and exacerbated loneliness, depression, anxiety, and suicide, among other negative mental health phenomena. And it has done so due to a purposeful design for smartphones and computers that activates a vicious dopamine feedback loop in our brains, conditioning us to expect more messages, texts, and other signals it interprets as *rewards*.

While no one is immune, children and those who've grown up as *digital natives* are particularly susceptible to the effects of this highly addictive feedback loop. It's hardly surprising, then, that Steve Jobs banned iPhones for his kids or that the children of Silicon Valley tech moguls often attend Waldorf schools, where such tech is prohibited and traditional instruction takes place.

As millennials, we've lived through a significant evolution of shorthand language owing to progression from AOL Instant Messenger to e-mail to texting to the endless riches of the Urban Dictionary. Through a constant stream, even barrage, of signals and information, we have come to use language that is unpolished, quick (to the point of being terse), transactional, and direct, even as it may convey a great deal of context—even nuance—through neologisms, novel syntax, grammar, acronyms, hashtags, emojis, symbols—everything but the digital kitchen sink.

And this is, despite and separate from, the relative stability of professional language among corporate employees in most workplaces (other than start-ups with a majority of Silicon Valley *bros* who speak like frat brothers) run or populated mostly by millennials. This is especially true for corporations, which have at most adjusted the language of their PR and customer experience (CX) efforts, if not so much their employee experience (EX), to reflect the newfangled language of social media.

And yet, the vernacular shorthand has actually opened the doors to innovative ways to express a multitude of emotions, context, and syntax in 140 characters, or at least with fewer words and syllables. Classicists and English majors everywhere hee and haw that digitally native millennials have *bastardized* the English language beyond recognition. But the picture is more complex than that.

When we look at similarly rapid evolutions of language we realize that unlike the much more conservative linguistic stratum of the academy or the Catholic Church, for example, language has always evolved much more quickly in the street or market, through daily usage and various sorts of shorthand, over millennia.

It's difficult to trace whether a shorter and shorter average attention span has come about *because of* technological advances like ICQ and Instant Messenger or vice versa. Twitter, of course, shortened discourse on its platform to 140 characters, later expanding it to 280. Facebook made it super easy to share emojis and graphics interchange format (GIF) images, which often condense the conversation to an exchange of memes.

This is not the language of nuance of cleverness, per se. After all, public intellectuals have gone the way of the Dodo bird in our age.

But don't mistake the speed or (the often ugly) efficiency of communication through acronyms, hashtags, urban slang, a few characters, emojis, or GIFs for a *dumbing down* or loss of nuance. It is simply the shifting of nuance to different modes (and nodes) of communication.

While the geeks, poets, nerds, and other misfits who see themselves as guardians of the integrity of the English language have more outlets for their creative works in the online ether, their cultural cachet, or for that matter social currency, has dramatically dropped in value since the heyday of Mailer, Roth, Bellow, and Wolff.

If anything, English has continued expanding and evolving in the same spongious manner that it always has, adding elements from all sorts of niche sublanguages, as well as, for the last two decades, increasing terminology from legalese, corporatese, and tech and finance language. Call it the ultimate Nerd's Revenge.

With the increasing presence of artificial intelligence (AI) and machine learning (ML) in everyday life, including in various apps for e-mail (auto-fill), texting (auto-correct), and messaging (Messenger bots), the effort required to communicate with others is getting smaller and smaller on the way to essentially zero. As the machines and software we use to communicate learn more and more about our language patterns, they will predictively communicate with customers, family, and others in preset ways that run on their own.

While many techies and coders may rejoice at the prospect of removing barriers around—and perfecting through prediction and automation—language and customer psychology, a scenario where machines are communicating among themselves to get work done instead of people is closer than we think.

No wonder that there's an evergreen conversation about a Digital Sabbath in tech, plus all sorts of IRL efforts (themed dinners, Tough Mudder events, curated travel, and others) to shake people out of tech addiction and their curmudgeonly ways exacerbated by instant communication and access to information —and increasingly, experiences through virtual reality (VR) and augmented reality (AR).

But before we trail off about some inevitably vicious cycle or doomsday scenario, let's remember that the media loves telling just-so stories, which are often not truly representative of facts on the ground.

Such is the case with millennials at work and other *adulting* activities. After all, armed with our overeducated, anxiously neurotic, values-first worldview and risk aversion, we tend to approach everything from career development, marriage, raising kids, buying a house, even picking just the right restaurant or cupcake bakery with a certain pragmatic savvy and experience-first mentality. This generally involves due diligence, research, filtering away the noise, asking our close networks for advice, and getting input (advice, coaching, etc.) from experts before making big decisions.

In short, even if we don't yet know the language and psychology of a new phase in life (marriage, kids, new job in a new industry), we are quick to learn, adopt, and leverage it out of necessity, rather than force our own language and psychology on the intended audience, which still tends toward Gen X or boomers, who are in most positions of leadership, funding, and authority. This is changing, even if we are still years away from the inflection point toward millennials becoming the majority in the said positions of power and authority.

***

One critical linguistic and psychological trend that millennials in the United States have lived through and embraced is the subtle, if critical, shift in language use and mentality from a more superficial, celebratory, forward-looking, folksy yet polished and masculine way of speaking and thinking that strives to project perfection and victory and bottles up imperfections and pain and suppresses anything contrary to itself to a more unfiltered, victim- and reckoning-focused, vulnerable, reactive, hyper-partisan language and psychology.

Today, we live in a world that pits, on the one hand, liberal intersectionality, checked privilege, overly sensitive, victimhood-focused, plaintiff lawyer's language that's largely defensive and feminine and couched in linguistic safe spaces to protect from a constellation of micro-aggressions against, on the other hand, the conservative, red-blooded, Bible values signaling, heartland-centered, exceptionalist narrative that's male, macho and unapologetically elitist, sexist, and traditional, sports-and-beer-loving, in a virtual, unending fight to the death.

Imagine going from the All-American *Golden Age* of Sports Center and Clinton's sex scandals in the 1990s where (too) many original sins were still forgiven to an America today that is sharply divided along the lines of politics, gender, race, sexual orientation, future prospects, and various others.

This shift has coincided with a transition from Clinton-era celebration over winning the Cold War and unprecedented geopolitical stability, combined with sustained economic growth and a tech boom, to a second Bush era full of terrorist attacks, ubiquitous surveillance and the rise of a militarized police, increasingly partisan politics, and increasingly expensive education and unaffordable housing, a time of widening inequality and then deep recession.

This was followed by a slow and unequal Obama recovery for all those but the 1 percent, with tremendous hope for meaningful change tempered by political obstructionism, a Wall Street released essentially scot-free from its crimes and misdemeanors because of a lack of political will, plus a sustained economic expansion, which has brought with it a series of new bubbles about to explode, including those of student debt, real estate, and others.

Our epoch is schizophrenic in the sense that there is a stark contrast between what we are told life is by the media versus how life is, in objective actuality. We complain more than ever, even though many aspects of our lives are better than they have ever been.

On the one hand, the average American lifestyle is at an all time high (at least on paper) for the ability to cure and prevent disease, get a world-class education for cheap or even free (online), start a business with essentially zero overhead, travel the world in record time and on a budget, find most any information instantly, communicate and collaborate easily with people all over world in different languages and time zones, as well as choose how we spend our time as humans and as employees, express our opinions to mass audiences with a click through any medium we wish, bring groups of people together instantly for any reason (or none, at all), and enjoy many freedoms afforded to us by living in a capitalist democracy.

On the other hand, we spend much of our day comparing ourselves to others on social media and growing anxious; chained to our smartphone and answering an endless stream of messages from everywhere; consumed with worries about our future, finances and careers, the effects of global warming, political stalemate, terrorist attacks that are of statistically insignificant probability, a long commute, looking good and rich and leisurely on Instagram, buying the latest gadgets, where to get the best cup of Cat's Ass (yes, really) coffee in town, and how to get the best baguettes and mozzarella for dinner, and all sorts of other First World problems.

Sure enough, there are most certainly real and grave problems we face like paying off student debt, taking care of aging parents, saving enough for retirement, and being able to pay off medical bills without bankruptcy. But by and large these problems are still smaller and much less than existential in comparison with those our fellow millennials often face in the developing world. In others words, we've ought to "put up and shut up" and feel lucky to be Americans.

Or at least that is what wealthy white males in power would have us think. And there's just the rub.

The blessing of being millennial is that we have at our disposal so many important elements in our lives having to do with living in a capitalist democracy that affords us not just political and personal freedoms, but the tremendous, unprecedented tools to create a productive, healthy, wealthy, and meaningful life for ourselves and our families. This is what accounts for our relative optimism about life.

The curse of being millennial is poor expectation management. We were raised in boom times with the expectation of a healthy, stable existence with solid prospects for a better life than our parents, as long as we followed the rules our parents and Gen X siblings had followed themselves to make a life and livelihood.

But the rules of the game (meaning the traditional process for moving up in life—careerwise, financially, in living one's best life, becoming the best version of oneself, in growing one's influence, and in achieving a lasting impact) completely changed as we grew up, enough for us to realize that the game is quite often rigged for those already born ahead in life.

Many of us got stuck on—or thrown off—the escalator for a while before getting back on, while others chose to take an entirely different path (entrepreneurship). This is what accounts for our clear-eyed pragmatism and savvy in finding our way through hype to reality, or creating that reality ourselves.

With this *A Tale of Two Cities* paradigm ("It was the best of times, it was the worst of times . . .") causing an impasse for those waiting for Trump and the gerontocracy to pass, millennials have hardly rested on their laurels or remained passive.

Using the massive wealth of channels to communicate and express themselves, millions of millennials have taken the initiative to blog; vlog; create podcasts and immersive plays, art, software, as well as all sorts of successful businesses, as well as to coach, consult, and train others in getting results more quickly in career, life, and business. In short, we've taken the initiative to create our own languages and mindsets, to give back to the world in our own ways.

And through the barrage of PR/media, fake news, and all sorts of misleading and outright false signals from people fronting happiness and wealth on social media to cover their anxiety, an entire stratum of millennial authors, entrepreneurs, podcasters, and other creatives—even marketers—have made a strategic decision to open their proverbial kimonos, bare their souls, and build their brands on top of great storytelling that includes the many ups and downs of life and business.

Authors like Mark Manson, Alex Banayan, Gary John Bishop, and Sean Whalen have used hard-edge storytelling based on their own hard-knock life experience to help people learn the "subtle art of not giving a f*ck," "find the third door," "unf*ck themselves," and "make sh*t happen," respectively (see https://www.amazon.com/Mark-Manson/e/B00BIJO-MOC/ref=sr_ntt_srch_lnk_6?qid=1532266645&sr=1-6; https://www.amazon.com/Alex-Banayan/e/B07933YVF1%3Fref=dbs_a_mng_rwt_scns_share; https://www.amazon.com/Gary-John-Bishop/e/B01M-9F5EEN; https://www.amazon.com/Sean-Whalen/e/B079K2BWC7). Apparently, the more cursing, the easier to get your point across these days.

This goes against the *grind and hustle* dogma perpetuated by the likes of Gary Vaynerchuk, Elon Musk, and other media and tech moguls pushing the premise of mindless hard work at the expense of personal development outside of business. This language and psychology is just a variant of the same *bro language* prevalent in finance, the sort of thing that leads to the infamous *humblebrag* (see https://melmagazine.com/en-us/story/rise-grind-and-ruin-the-dangerous-fetishization-of-hustle-porn; https://www.businessinsider.com/phrases-only-wall-street-understands-2014-1; https://www.merriam-webster.com/dictionary/humblebrag).

The focus of the aforementioned authors' work is to empower the amateur who feels himself way out of his league in business and life to find his voice, embrace a lack of knowledge, and learn through an immersive experience of building and iterating, making mistakes and learning forward from them.

Millennial directness is definitely a *thing*. Born of fast communication, disillusionment, and the outsized desire to create change in a broken world stacked against us, it is both a necessity and a style of living and being. So is the amateur's chutzpah, born of necessity's ingenuity and a distrust of authority figures, textbooks, and outmoded ways of seeing and learning the worldview we were spoon-fed in school and college (even grad school).

What isn't on Google or Wikipedia must be built from scratch or experienced in person.

And so, while the Left and Right fight on in politics and older generations on both sides keep bashing us for every earthly ill, we millennials just keep on keeping on with our life plans, patiently creating a culture as every other generation has, using our own language and mindset.

Being still relatively young and risk averse, on average, we're doing our best with a lack of choices and safety net, working hard to create the right conditions to survive any future recessions, political crises, or macro-geopolitical events.

***

When it comes to the language companies use to attract millennials and get us to open our hearts and wallets, it is usually sincere, concise, and mission-driven language that speaks to us and our values. It's hardly surprising that in our age of hyper-partisanship and division, company CEOs often have to take a stand on social issues, whereas they have studiously avoided doing so in the past, to avoid controversy and loss of market share and brand value.

One great case in point is the shunning, then embrace of Colin Kaepernick by Nike as a spokesman for the injustice and discrimination faced for decades by African Americans all over the country in the criminal justice system and from militarized police forces shooting to kill, rather than defuse situations. While Nike may have lost some conservative customers disagreeing with their message in 2018, they gained market share and a big bump in sales from launching a campaign featuring him.

Companies from across the spectra of financial services, consumer goods, food and beverages, automotive, and others have understood—and implemented, with varying success—the language we understand best, which is that of great user/customer/employee experience, a simple and clean user interface, alignment on (a generally more progressive) social mission and values, great design over flashiness, healthier rather than unhealthy, providing a great experience above all and leaving a positive impact on the earth and others, rather than just showing off.

As for any age cohort, the language companies use for millennials is always evolving, depending on economic cycles, changing sensibilities, and with the rise of spending power with age and status (see https://www2 .deloitte.com/insights/us/en/topics/marketing-and-sales-operations/ millennials-x-z-beyond-generational-marketing-consumer-profiling.html).

For now, experience is king. As Carl W. Buehner once said, "People may not remember exactly what you did, or what you said, but they will always remember how you made them feel" (see https://www.goodreads.com/quotes/8937381-people-may-forget-what-you-say-they-may-forget-what).

***

Summary

Language—what is the type of language we use, expect to see from companies we love and buy from and work for; what is the messaging that resonates with us (and works for us to buy or invest in a brand or interaction)?

CHAPTER 7

Millennials at Work

Us poor millennials.[1] We're generation screwed—by school debt, the economy, in politics, and by our boomer, Gen X bosses. We have become a sort of inconvenient truth inside the working world.

Job-hoppers, narcissists, attention/trophy seekers, needy over-sharers, we've been called them all. Not a day goes by without another article in mainstream media overanalyzing us, trying to make sense of us, prescribing the perks to attract us, bewailing our rise to majority working demographic by 2020. A cottage industry exists explaining us to companies, consulting on how to deal with us, attract us, keep us, coax us every way, and so on.

Well, here we are. The time of reckoning is here. It's time to set the record straight. What do we want from work?

As a millennial myself who's worked in law and finance, tech and health care—both for large corporations and small start-ups—I've seen the spectrum from the great to awful in a company's approach to attracting, managing, and retaining its millennial talent. Aside from Google, Facebook, Apple, and a couple dozen giants, large corporations typically are slow and tone-deaf to adjust incentives and benefits to attract top talent. Too many start-ups simply chase the latest perks without much thought to long-term practices that keep the best employees in.

What Is It That We Want from Work, in Short?

According to *Harvard Business Review*, in descending order of importance, we want to have our work mean something, to solve problems with the

---

[1]Reprinted with permission from *Forbes*, https://www.forbes.com/sites/forbescoaches council/2016/12/01/how-to-attract-and-retain-millennials-and-get-them-to-do-their-lifes-best-work-for-you/#15900f8c4e70

environment and society, interact with cool and interesting people, find prestige in the company we work for, do work we're passionate about, become an expert, maintain work–life balance, progress in our careers, achieve financial security, and start our own businesses.

As it turns out, this is quite similar to [the wants of] all the other generations before us, with some variation.

There's more to actuality than surveys can appreciate, however. There's the experience of life and that of coaching.

A culture of *gigs*, not jobs and sharing versus owning as the norm have seeped into the ethos of this generation. Those unpaid internships and portfolio careers are normal; loyalty, an artifact. Changing careers is common and has never been so easy. Just hire a coach, and make the move in weeks.

Perhaps the difference between millennials and past generations is the speed of change, not underlying motivations or desires. Everyone wants a dream job, but we millennials expect it. Because we are so quick to move, we want our job performance feedback now, *or else*. We treasure openness, transparency, ethics, and social impact.

These are the lofty standards we hold our employers to. While there is ever greater progress by employers (and our laws) to tackle the ills of yesteryear (like the gender wage gap and the spectrum of discrimination), reality is all too often incompatible with vision.

As always, there's inherent tension between duty to the company and self. Not all the work we do can possibly be interesting each day, each week. Yet clearly, there is consciousness among HR professionals that something different must be done to keep, not just attract millennials.

The Zappos companies of the world attempt a flat hierarchy, while the Gravity Payments standardize their salaries. Valiant, but largely fruitless efforts, all, in my opinion.

What's Worked and What Has Flopped? Let's Take a Look

One start-up trend is unlimited vacation, but who can take advantage of this when nobody wants to be the first to fly? What can free snacks do for your future aside from making you fat? The foosball tables will just stand there without use. Those open floor plans? A nuisance to real productivity.

More effective perks and benefits include free health care and proactive management thereof, employer student loan repayment and tuition reimbursement, 401(k) matches from Day 1, regular feedback on performance, and quarterly company retreats and monthly town halls to get all employees to hear how things are going, what is being done, and the strategy and tactics of each function and effort. Tech budgets for each newbie, dedicated time for outside projects, plus internal hackathons—all this builds trust, loyalty, and new ideas that can grow into streams of revenue.

Not every perk or benefit is scalable or economically tenable for every company. While health and money management are key, each company must look beyond the obvious to keep its best. But transparency on company and personal performance is essential. Commitment to good health (financial as much as physical); a smarter, wiser team; great tech; sustained career development and coaching; and fair compensation are the start of thoughtful and effective human capital management for millennials. Some companies have even started to encourage taking jobs outside to gain a different perspective, only to hire such employees back in.

In such a paradigm, *skin in the game* exists, and all the big incentives are aligned.

Like us or not, millennials are here to stay. The companies that lure us in must do a better job of keeping us by asking each of us directly (not the *experts*) what we really want and need from work, learning about the values we espouse, leaving us room to do things our way, giving us the resources and leverage to let us do our life's best work.

Those that succeed will reap not only breakneck innovation but cross-pollination between industries, worldviews, cultures, and technologies—plus new ways of doing business. Everyone wins this way. The ones that fail to *get us* will not keep us and will fall behind and ultimately fail.

And in the end, worker millennials are also consumers—and we know we're king.

Entitled? Maybe. Crazy? Like a fox.

***

What do millennials want from work? As we've discussed at length, millennials want just about the same exact things that all other generations before us have wanted, including psychological safety, genuine friendships with colleagues, the chance to achieve good results, build self-esteem, gain the respect of others and for others.

The difference with other generations is that millennials have been much more vocal (others would call this *entitled*) about these demands, buttressed by a high employment rate in a candidate's market, whereas the older generations are more conservative and higher up the leadership chain, on average, simply by virtue of age and career stage.

We've talked at length about the direct connection of values from our life that we want to see reflected in our workplace. We seek morality, creativity, problem solving, spontaneity, lack of prejudice, help with paying off student debt, getting affordable housing, doing our life's best work in a company we love, which pays well and helps us grow quickly as people and professionals, plus helps us build an amazing career and life.

While much has been written about work–life *balance* over the years, there's a stronger trend toward work–life *integration* for millennials, which is more attuned to the realities of the speed of business, portfolio careers, the ability to work flexibly, even nomadically without losing productivity or poorly affecting the bottom line.

In this vein, rather than commute to and from an office every day for 2 hours or more, many (perhaps most of us) would much rather be able to work from home or a coffee shop without a micromanaging boss breathing down our neck.

Whether or not some of us actually *need* that micromanaging boss behind us, helping guide us, depends on the business and the employee. Either way, we don't want to work with assholes and prefer the company to have a formal or informal No Asshole Rule.

Life is too short and there are too many great companies out there doing work we care about, for us to work with and alongside people who don't share our values, on something we don't care about. Plus, at least for the time being, the economy is too good for us not to shop around for better companies, titles, and compensation, if we can. And yes, we can, and do.

There are numerous reasons, perfectly valid and intelligent reasons, why millennials tend to switch jobs, even if it's at similar rates and for similar reasons as everyone else at the same career stage. These include staying fresh, relevant, and grounded; learning new skills; getting paid more and having a better title; and building a brand, network, and portfolio more quickly, among others.

It is also helpful that the stigma of short tenure has largely gone, given the gig economy and the massive demand for talent that isn't matched by the supply from the market of available talent. More than anything, a large proportion of us feel little to no loyalty for companies that talk the talk, but don't walk the walk on issues as important as diversity and inclusion, wage equality, promotion practices, parental leave, work–life integration, moral business practices, personal development, not being evil, and a host of other (mostly progressive) issues important to us.

Nobody is leaving because there's no craft coffee or beer at work or because nobody bought a foosball table. It's the big-picture stuff that matters, but the picture includes many more themes than for previous generations at our stage. Gen X and boomers likely wanted all the same things, but were either afraid to ask or had no leverage to do so without high cost.

Perhaps the most important locus of work issues faced by many millennials right now is around the transition from more technical, individual contributor roles in their early to mid-career to leadership positions where they are responsible for managing people, facing clients, and making strategic decisions that dramatically impact company success, culture, and the bottom line.

To help in this transition, management should spend meaningful time and resources on coaching millennial new managers and leaders on existing company culture; the fundamentals of empathy; giving regular feedback; celebrating small wins; engagement through vulnerability and storytelling; detecting signs of burnout and combating it; choosing and utilizing the best combination of benefits for them to ensure physical, mental, and financial health; creating and managing personal development plans for employees, as well as around personal branding (LinkedIn profile, executive presence, public speaking, presenting, selling, networking effectively, etc.) for each team member and themselves.

Such coaching by managers is helpful, but not nearly enough if done ad hoc. The simple truth is that most managers have no idea how to coach people effectively, and no software, online course, or webinar training can magically help them become effective managers.

As such, they can always use help from outside coaches and trainer trainers who provide a fresh eye, diagnostic tools, and proven methodologies to help managers get the best out of their teams and individuals. At the very least, managers should try coaching each other first in a non-threatening, safe environment before trying the same on their employees.

The elements of coaching that can be automated by software are effective feedback (both anonymous and direct), personal development planning (with IRL updates and discussions), and the 360-degree review (together with in-person meetings), as well as all issues of project management, scheduling, and resource access.

More than just helping people become their best self through coaching and personal development, it's just as important to create a workplace that optimizes physical and mental health for each employee, beyond just through accessibility and benefit selection plus utilization.

To design a physical workplace that keeps millennials and all other employees physically and mentally healthy, as well as productive and performing at their peak, while building a culture of health first, profitability second, companies need to focus on three main areas: space design, organizational design, and life design.

For workplace design, employees need natural light throughout the year; a mix of private, public, team, and breakout spaces (as opposed to just the open floor design, which is a disaster for productivity); more bathroom access for women than men; office walkability; access to outdoor space with trees, plants, and walking paths; dedicated booths for taking phone calls; a kitchen stocked with water, high-quality coffee, and healthy snacks; a common area separate from the work area where employees can ideally mingle with employees of other teams and companies.

While many companies like Google, Apple, and Facebook have doubled down on centralizing life for employees on a corporate campus, the truth remains that flexible (especially remote) work arrangements are of great importance to millennials, who often have awful commutes and can't afford rents in neighborhoods closer to work.

Even more importantly, millennials find work–life integration critical, since it allows them to be flexible on hours worked even while maintaining productivity.

In short, employers should not invest more than necessary in expensive real estate and beautiful offices, but rather make flexible arrangements available, including working from coworking spaces like WeWork, as well as from coffee shops or home offices. This exact strategy netted Cisco massive savings in real estate costs and increased employee engagement. For now, many companies are still experimenting with flexible work arrangements and it's already clear that for many employees who are not as self-starting as their peers, they require more face time at the office.

As such, there will always be employees who prefer to come into the office for precious face time with the boss and their team. As such, in terms of ergonomics, employers should look to provide employees with sit stand desks, encourage them to use staircases when possible for increased movement and health, and provide dedicated relaxation areas where employees can take short naps and otherwise take a meaningful break at least a couple of times a day.

Biophilic office design principles—meaning the placement of plants throughout the office, as well as maximizing views of nature and natural light—have shown to increase productivity. Using technology that is minimally straining to the eye while remaining aesthetically pleasing is also important to an office environment that is healthy and conducive to productivity and peak performance.

When it comes to organizational design, recent years have brought many experiments with mixed or little success, whether around paying everyone an effective "minimum wage" of $70,000 per year (as at Gravity Payments) or instituting a completely flat hierarchy (as at Zappos). Some like Deutsche Bank have tried co-CEOs and failed miserably. CEOs and leaders like Michael Bloomberg, Larry Ellison, Sergey Brin, and Arnold Schwarzenberg have attracted attention for paying themselves a $1 salary, but for the most part, this is a symbolic camaraderie with workers that feels hollow, since most such CEOs receive stock compensation, and are, for the most part, already billionaires in the 0.01 percent of accumulated wealth. Such gestures are little consolation for the common line worker or entry level analyst.

Without taking sides in the CEO versus worker pay ratio debate, optics do matter for morale. Yet, our focus here isn't so much on optics, as much as good design.

According to a study by PwC, 10 factors underpin great organizational design that aligns well with corporate strategy. These include not dwelling on the past and its foibles, designing with the company *DNA* or *special sauce* squarely in mind, fixing the structure last (as opposed to first, as is the temptation), optimizing how the company utilizes talent, focusing on the factors under control, promoting accountability throughout the organization, benchmarking little (if at all), letting the formalities of lines and boxes in the org chart fit the company's purpose and mission, emphasizing the informal, and building on existing strengths.

The elements of the aforementioned most important to millennials are clarity on feeling and contributing the *special sauce* of company mission and the CEO's vision, optimizing how talent is best utilized with their career development and constant learning in mind, focus on execution (rather than the competition), informality in communication and dress, few or no benchmarks except for those of individual personal development, and few layers of hierarchy.

On the subject of life design, it is both a competitive necessity and a high return on investment (ROI) for companies to actively help their employees design their lives to enable them to become the best version of themselves as people and professionals. In the simplest sense, companies should strive to take away or minimize the main life stressors for their employees in order to help them focus on productivity and growth at work, rather than spend undue energy and resources on elements of their life where companies are better situated to assist with funds or resources.

Aside from flexible work arrangements, work–life integration, and working smarter facilitated by the latest tech with software and other productivity and collaboration tools, we've previously discussed implementing a benefit strategy that covers health, mental, dental, and accidental (so to speak) insurance, as well as financial well-being, a budget for learning and professional development, as well as for coaching and guidance regarding health, career, leadership, peak performance, life milestones, benefit utilization, and any other necessary critical subject, bringing in accountability, a timeline, and structure.

A mix of tech and the human touch throughout any of these processes goes a long way toward higher utilization and meaningful results, as well as toward helping the company find where investment into employee well-being and growth brings the highest ROI, so that limited resources are used optimally and achieve the results sought.

Regarding the commute, companies should both subsidize it and minimize it through flexible work arrangements, enabling face time, but not necessarily every day of the week.

For millennial parents, companies should provide a child care subsidy, if they're not able to provide child care on-site. For all millennial employees struggling with high rents, companies can either provide subsidized housing (think WeLive, Common) or otherwise help employees as an apartment guarantor with minimal cost and risk (TheGuarantors, Insurent, and others).

On a separate but equally meaningful track, companies should consider offering charitable matching for millennials looking to contribute pretax to nonprofit organizations they feel strongly about (CaringCent and others), as well as matching for micro-investing (think Stash, Acorn, Robin Hood) to help employees establish and grow their financial well-being.

***

While most HR and CFO-vertical executives usually gasp at the projected cost of what they see as a bald-faced *wishlist* for *needy* millennial employees, or at most acknowledge it with lip service, most have still not grasped the new *normal* of half the workforce being millennial starting with 2019.

Even more unfortunately, they often fail to appreciate the massive costs of turnover and short-term perks they provide on the basis of what others are doing, rather than spending the time to diagnose employee needs by speaking to them, then redirecting the funds they use for benefits and perks never used, which fail to retain and engage employees, into the kind of proactive, forward-looking benefit packages that will attract the best talent, keep, and develop it, thereby building a stronger brand, higher profit margins, and market position.

As the providers of last resort driven by the laws of supply and demand in a candidate-centered economy with record-low unemployment, low engagement, and high turnover, companies simply have no choice but to stop being reactive and start thinking proactively about how they approach their talent strategy. If they don't, they risk becoming a talent backwater and a declining brand, as well as simply going out of business.

Summary

Millennials at Work—what we like and don't like from our work; how and where we like doing it; how we see our place and contribution in the world; why we're so keen on working on problems we care about; why we change jobs and industries so often; what can be done to attract, then hire and retain us; how we participate in and fuel the gig economy and what it means for our medium- and long-term future; what is the future of work with millennials at the helm (in top executive roles); impact of increasing automation for the learned professions and the start-ups that service them

CHAPTER 8

Millennials and Life Planning/Design

We've spoken at length about millennial approaches to work, finances, marriage, and asset (home, auto) ownership.

To the extent that as a group we millennials know that our standard of living is on average lower than our parents' and our safety net is negligible and shrinking, the economy is inequitable and growing more so between the ultrarich and everyone else, we also know that rapid change (and often, the greater complexity that comes with it) in all areas of life is the only constant.

Our generation's life design is increased algorithmic automation or streamlining of many areas of life, including the home (Internet of Things), communication (messenger apps, FaceTime/Skype, and others); curated content of all forms (Amazon, Facebook, Instagram, Netflix, Hulu, HBO on Demand, Udemy, our varied news feeds, and many other forms and platforms); instant or quick delivery of services and goods (food, consumer goods, clothing, and many others). On the other hand, we bake in our yearning for meaningful human experiences (self-guided travel, eating out, curated networking events, etc.) over goods and *forced* experiences (schooling, career choices, going to a house of worship, or on guided trips with parents).

The latter comes as a reaction to growing up with an overabundance of *stuff* (consumer goods, toys, junk) that we didn't want or that made us nervous because it meant constantly comparing one's stash of stuff with that of others. The uncluttering and returning to *basics* might be described as almost a form of millennial spirituality.

Due to lingering anxiety about the future, as well as decreased loyalty to employers, there is a widespread desire to hedge one's bets, keep one's options open, create other streams of revenue outside of one's *day job,* and minimize the risk of disappointment by crowdsourcing advice from one's high-value network on everything from travel, service providers, food, and a range of other experiences.

The hedging behavior is also evident in a large proportion of millennials investing in cryptocurrency, as well as micro-investing in their own savings and trading accounts (Stash/Acorn and Robin Hood) and micro-donating through platforms like CaringCent, as mentioned in Chapter 7.

And in the same vein, accessing, researching, and sorting through a wide variety of information and options before making a decision, big or small, about almost anything has never been easier, thanks to Google, homes serviced by Alexa or Google Home, wired through by the Internet of Things, as well as the easy input from one's network, often spread around the country and the world.

Due to the reputation, employment, business, and other risks inherent in expressing one's even slightly controversial opinions (especially those that are seen as conservative, given the solidly liberal political bent of the *average* millennial), which may be seen and shared by people outside of one's immediate network on any platform, the majority of millennials generally find comfort in expressing or parroting the liberal opinions and views of themselves or those of like mind. Most others stay silent to avoid the risk of misinterpretation and adverse downstream consequences. One need look no further than the periodic circulation of *unfriend* requests on Facebook by those intolerant of friends voting for Trump, supporting conservative causes, or otherwise holding views substantially different from their own.

The spread of *fake news,* fake online reviews, and instant, self-righteous outrage over every sort of triviality, issue, and talking point in the media and politics, as well as IRL interactions, has only further eroded patience trust, the quality and depth of intellectual discourse, as well as incentive or desire to pursue the truth.

The algorithmic automation and constant targeting and retargeting of news, content, reviews, and ads based on user-shared (or hacked or unauthorized) data has created an echo chamber for all of us online, further splitting us into groups based on micro-tastes, business niches, political affiliations, donations to groups we support, sports we play, cars we drive, content we consume, and just about any other quantifiable categorization. These forces have made us more cynical, less responsive, less attentive, less patient, less united around a positive common cause, and less forthright with each other, as well as with ourselves.

The prevalent political correctness that has grown in force over our millennial lifetimes, embracing on the one hand the Lesbian Gay Bisexual Trans-sexual and Queer (LGBTQ) movement and women's rights even while increasingly shouting down conservative (even centrist) views, has perpetuated a sort of necessary, hypocritical doublespeak among many millennials, a deepening contrast between views expressed online and IRL, between the values they espouse in conversation and the values they actually defend in practice (if at all).

On the other hand, the conservative backlash to political correctness has, in part, led to the escalation of rhetoric and political activity of both the right and left fringes, resulting in part in the reactionary wave of support for both President Donald Trump and far-left progressives, who are inching closer to the mainstream among Democrats.

The reason this mainstreaming of both political fringes matters is that it has uncovered and increasingly popularized an essential disregard for truth (and often, justice, fairness, and the rule of law), which has a way of further pitting generations, contractual and political parties against each other in a way that seeks to *score points* at the expense of consensus, compromise, and long-term socioeconomic stability. In short, when the loudest few voices consistently shout down the silent, moderate majority on both sides, free speech, group membership, and democratic participation are chilled due to the risks to career, family, business, and other critical components of life in a capitalist democracy.

We have seen the very real risks of free speech for conservative employees of Google and many others who were fired for it, as well as for high school students protesting for gun control and Dr. Ford, Brett Kavanaugh's accuser, who have experienced death threats galore.

The mainstreaming of political fringes likewise breeds escapism and at most armchair participation in political and social life, hardly due to apathy, but rather to the aforementioned risks involved.

And as such, it's hardly surprising that millennials are more likely than previous generations to avoid conflict and controversy. We have been coddled by our parents, humbled by the Great Recession, and prevented from healthy conflict resolution and argumentation habits by technology, trolls, and evolving societal norms.

In a fundamental sense, millennials are the *wait cursor* generation, conditioned in childhood to wait their turn and pay their dues while getting their degrees and stable jobs, whose value evaporated in the recession, then to withhold *unsafe* opinions for fear of offending others and ruination, who have had to hustle like crazy, work side gigs and create portfolio careers, all the while maintaining the image that their operating system is still loading and installing new patches.

As happens with every generation, there is an expiration date for political correctness and withholding oneself from public conversations and political participation, no matter the costs.

Our spending power is large and growing and we are gaining influence IRL from career progression, increasing asset ownership, more profound decision-making power in more areas of life, and meaningful, sustained political participation.

The coming few years will see a mass bloom of millennials coming into their own in all areas of life—belatedly, but with great energy and force. Sheer demographics and so many young people finally finding their voice in a stagnant political and pop culture will continue to transform not just technology and business, but workplace and political dynamics, among others.

And with this paradigm shift, millennial life design will also continue evolving, largely in the same predictable way that all generations have always adapted to starting a family, moving to the suburbs, buying assets and investing, then voting and spending their interests.

Even if we won't be quite as well off, in relative terms, as our parents or Gen Xers, we will adapt and find our own way to live and reinvent the American Dream.

***

Summary

Millennials and Life Planning/Design—how we plan out (or fail to plan) our finances; marriage and family life; home, auto, and other asset ownership; travel, among other life-cycle and milestone events

CHAPTER 9

Customer Experience for Millennials

The Importance of Customer Experience in the Age of Instant Gratification[1]

There is much talk these days about the rise of customer experience (CX). Nearly every service, product, or expertise is first hiveminded, Uberized, and Yelped, then tweeted with true glee or scorn, ordered hands free thanks to Alexa, coupon coded, and reviewed to death. Instant vilification kills and instant gratification buoys brands—with just a click. Whatever room for error may have existed before our digital nativity is now razor-thin.

Moving into New Digital Ground

As customers, being jerked around by telecoms, car rental companies, and airlines is passé. Last year, after an Avis rental problem was poorly handled, I did some Google research and reached out to a customer service executive. I had a callback and refund within 24 hours. A Delta kosher meal debacle in the spring was quickly solved with gift cards to our mailbox. No-questions-asked refunds (think Trader Joe's and Amazon) have now become the norm, rather than the exception.

---

[1]Reprinted with permission from Forbes. August, 2017. 'The Importance of Customer Experience in the Age of Instant Gratification.' https://www.forbes.com/sites/forbescoachescouncil/2017/08/08/the-importance-of-customer-experience-in-the-age-of-instant-gratification/#32120a6b60e1

But CX is not just cleaning up a mess efficiently or sharing information nicely. The journey of a customer begins in the foothills of the psyche.

A *need* or *want* is crystallized inside the mind—a vacation, an iPhone, maybe a piece of software. After a search on Google, sorting through a plethora of options and possibly more research, a choice and eventually a purchase, rental or exchange are made. The product or service is received and used. If broken, a fix or refund is initiated instantly. If the experience is good, engagement with the brand continues, with or without feedback. If things go south, the customer may leave and make a fuss or disengage quite passively.

Standing Out from the Noise

To reach and engage a customer, brands must deliver one or several of the following: novelty; delight; a form of greater health or wealth; improvement in a business process through cost or time savings; increase in quality, organization, or convenience; and/or a vision or mission that compels the customer to take action, whether in the form of a purchase or gainful influence with others.

By definition, large corporations have figured out a working funnel to direct a customer from *need* to *purchase*. The savvy ones devote a wealth of resources and manpower to optimizing every stage and process constantly—from ads, sponsorships, (sear engine optimization (SEO), and social media to customer relationship management software (CRMs), user interface (UI), user experience (UX), and application program interfaces (APIs), and from sales scripts, retargeting, shopping carts, and up-sells to payment processing, onboarding, returns, and exchanges.

Early-stage start-ups, restricted by their lack of funds and time, must choose which element to focus on and which to leave aside for later. Tech start-ups often choose to differentiate themselves by focusing on great UI/UX or catchy copy (e.g., Oscar and Casper), customer success (e.g., Buffer and early Zappos), driving sales (e.g., BounceX, Persado), breakthrough tech (e.g., Cortica, MobileODT), or raising massive funds (e.g., Juicero).

Raising Social Conscience

Nontechy, mission-driven outfits sometimes let their products do the talking.

World Wide Hearing, for example, supplies low-cost hearing aids to children in the developing world. Imagine hearing how the world sounds for the first time.

Solight Design has patented its low-cost solar pop-up lanterns. Whether you're a soldier in Afghanistan or a hurricane survivor in Mississippi, you can open up a lantern in the black of night, far off the grid (it charges in the sun) for an instant source of light—without the safety hazards of fire, smoke, and kerosene.

Both products, based on social conscience, lead with great design, a critical function that both delights and changes lives, all equating to a *wow* effect. Add to this a commitment from the entire team—from management on down—to help each user succeed, and you get sustained delight, plus awesome feedback from users.

Turning CX into a Science

While CX is often seen as an art, there's a push to codify it into a science. In the past few years, a handful of CX certificate programs has sprung up, including at Rutgers, Stanford Graduate School of Business (GSB), and Arizona State University (ASU). (Disclaimer: I'm an advisory board member for the Rutgers program.)

These programs seek to help large enterprises and small start-ups train new chief customer experience officers (CCXOs) to see CX as a gateway to true innovation, greater profits, better net promoter scores, fewer refunds, proactive (rather than reactive) social media engagement, repeat buyers, higher prices, bigger purchase sizes, and so on.

Getting CX right is no longer a luxury, but a critical business priority. Just ask United, with its squall of bad PR after a man was dragged off a flight, and a large rabbit died in a cargo hold.

Reinventing Your Crisis Strategy

Lawyering up and adding a PR spin is no longer a valid crisis strategy, even for big brands like United. Neither is crisis management over social media alone. The same old CX no longer works. Between the speed of righteous indignation and its many outlets by consumers, a fallout from a screwup can now destroy a company.

How do you arm your brand against such fate? Pay heed to the (often misunderstood) millennial consumer. Be human, transparent, and acknowledge when you fail. Make sure to have a social conscience and think twice about your impact and carbon footprint.

Just as important, espouse your mission and your values every day. Solve problems right away and make sure to follow up, repeatedly and consistently until resolution and delight. Confirm each customer is meaningfully better off for interacting with your brand. If you can't help directly, find a way to help them through your trusted partners. And just as importantly, make sure to *hire* people who know your customers, because they *are* your customers or see the world in the same way as them. This way, you'll learn the tides of customer behavior in advance—but only if you listen well and consistently.

***

With a lifetime spending power estimated at $10 trillion, millennials are poised to be not just the largest generation ever, but also a massive opportunity for business owners.

The most important front where brands compete for millennial customers is CX. Rather than just a business's reaction to a customer complaint or question (customer service), CX is all about the lifetime of interactions between brand and customer, meaning many different touchpoints from well before any purchase is made until well after the product or service is used.

The nature and quality of those multiple touchpoints are judged by digitally native, restless, and impatient millennials with regard to speed and ease of use; intuitive, clean, and delightful UI/UX; always on, easily reached, highly responsive, and always excellent customer service; active and relevant presence across all major social platforms (Facebook, Instagram, Snapchat, Pinterest, LinkedIn, etc.); authenticity or genuineness and the degree of delight (or lack thereof) in the experience of brand/service/product discovery.

A brand must not only be transparent about its mission and values, but also agile to change at the speed of business and shifting customer tastes, always looking to engage and collaborate with its millennial customers, rather than research them through focus groups.

As we can see from the explosion of every kind of subscription boxes (BirchBox, BarkBox, and a thousand others), as well as the exploding popularity of unboxing videos in recent years, delight and wonder in the experience of a product and brand are critical for millennials (see https://www .inc.com/christina-desmarais/heres-data-showing-the-crazy-growth-of-subscription-box-services-infographic.html; https://qz.com/quartzy/1374703/ unboxing-videos-will-take-over-the-world).

It's also the same wonder and experience that millennials hope to share with their friends IRL and on social media, so the brand must not disappoint or risk the wrath of viral condemnation. Make a customer look good and smart in front of friends, and you've got a fan for life.

We've discussed at length the importance of increasingly AI-driven algorithms—and the suggestion engines they power—to every sort of research and purchasing decision made by millennials, including products on Amazon, movies and shows on Netflix, potential connections on LinkedIn and Facebook, brands to follow on Instagram and Pinterest, doctors to choose on Zocdoc, among others.

The other, equally important piece of the research and decision making is crowdsourcing. In an age when reviews can be ordered easily or cooked to order by minions, it is most often the wisdom of one's posse or close group of friends with known tastes and standards that carries the greatest weight.

In lieu of strong opinions from one's close friends on FB or IRL, there is the (questionable, but influential) wisdom of (often paid) influencers. Influencers from Kim Kardashian with her tens of millions of followers on social media all the way down to micro-influencers, with just a pithy few hundred or thousand followers are enlisted by brands to engage their networks to pave the way to customer purchases through trust and verified testimonials and reviews.

Social proof—mention in top publications like *Forbes* and *Entrepreneur*, Inc. and *Fast Company*—is critical for new and aspiring brands, tech and otherwise, to overcome the skepticism of millennial customers, who are risk averse and looking for a superior experience in even small purchases like socks and underwear, sheets and toiletries. While such publications have cracked down on shameless plugs by paid writers, there are still many questionable practices employed by start-ups to get PR/media exposure for their brand for the benefit of lowering the barrier to competition with larger, more established brands (see http://thoughtforyourpenny.com/technology/interwebz/huffpost-shut-contributor-platform).

Comfort and a feeling of luxury elicited by a product and the ethical, sustainable practices of the brand that creates it are also critical. Certifications for sustainability, fair trade, greenness, Leadership in Energy and Environmental Design (LEED)-certified, organic, local production, artisan-ness, and others of a similar nature found in abundance in stores like Whole Foods and Trader Joe's are virtue and status signals, as well as obligatory declarations of mission and values by brands to draw in millennials keen to signal their own virtues and taste to their friends or potential mates.

More than just the presentation and signaling of a brand, many millennials are keen to experience a product or service for free before buying, whether that's a mattress (Casper and Purple), sheets (Brooklinen, CloudTen), coaching (free discovery call), performance-based marketing, or much anything else, as well as no-cost, no-frills returns (a la Amazon).

Due to a profusion of classic, reinvented, and *disruptive* brands all positioning for customers, plus a wide variety of messaging, cross-platform ad targeting and retargeting, as well as a rising volume of messages and ads across all platforms daily, the average attention span of a millennial browsing for a product or service online is quite short.

As such, a vicious cycle of ads, e-mails, multiple and growing customer touchpoints by e-mail, Facebook, Instagram, and elsewhere is necessary to compete in a crowded marketplace for products and services. Differentiation can come from humor, controversy, great storytelling, catchy characters or lines, or just by contrast in tone or message.

But no matter the context for each brand to compete, the emotional effect of experiencing a brand is the most important factor for engaging millennials and creating customers out of them. To some millennials, like all others, brand loyalty is everything with an emotional connection, or otherwise instantly dispensable when competing on price.

The key takeaway about CX is that above and beyond even values, quality, and emotion, the product or service sold by a brand must help the customer succeed in some tangible and meaningful way, making him or her look good, wise, and prescient—and also help him or her pass down the same feeling of success, value, and empowerment down the chain to others (see https://www.retaildive.com/news/millennials-seek-emotional-connections-before-purchasing/445545; https://www.chiefmarketer.com/what-it-really-takes-to-earn-millennial-loyalty; http://customerthink.com/customer-experience-and-customer-success-whats-the-difference).

Brands keen to compete on CX with others must take care to not just put their money where their mouth is, but to really get CX right, or else . . .

More than 2 years after a finding that 89 percent of brands planned to compete on the basis of CX, it turns out that only 30 percent of brands actually claim success in terms of differentiation or tangible benefits.

And finally, it turns out that the key to a good CX may actually lie in a great employee experience (EX), which gets employees aligned with mission and values, empowered to help customers succeed (not just troubleshoot) while helping promote themselves in their careers and lives.

In all, the secret to a great CX for millennials is the same as for all others—the people delivering it and their EX and how they communicate the brand's *special sauce* to customers and help them succeed in their respective journeys.

***

Summary

Customer Experience for Millennials—how we buy, how we evaluate options, how we experience products and services, how we think about customer service, how we think about customer success, what works (and what doesn't work) to reach and engage us

CHAPTER 10

The Brooklynization of Millennials

The Millennial Curation Wave Pushing Back against Automation[1]

Sir Peter Ustinov once famously said, "In America, through pressure of conformity, there is freedom of choice, but nothing to choose from" (see https://www.brainyquote.com/quotes/peter_ustinov_103982).

The state of informed choice in 2019 has never been more promising; yet, choice fatigue is slowly seeping in. The Internet has made available vast stores of information, analysis, and feedback to enable choosing smartly, every time—or so one would expect in a perfect world. And yet, the value of all open-source information is fast approaching zero. The sheer volume, scale, and speed of new content creation and delivery keeps growing every year.

Meanwhile, both time and our attention seem to shrink inversely. As humans, we require curation as a bare necessity. Before the prevalence of Wikipedia, WikiLeaks, and other resources tasked with making knowledge public, taste and information were elite controlled. Elite tastemakers would pronounce an *up or down* like Roman emperors of art and fashion, literature, technology, the news, and more.

Our age is hailed as the first to finally democratize these vast stores of information and content. The growing flood has made consumption an omnivore's dilemma with a dose of FOMO (fear of missing out).

---

[1]Reprinted with permission from *Forbes*, https://www.forbes.com/sites/forbescoaches-council/2017/09/14/the-millennial-curation-wave-pushing-back-against-automa-tion/#4e4b45278b03

Despite their equal opportunism, or perhaps because of it, large content platforms and their Mad Men minions have made intelligent curation de rigueur again. Taste making has, in large part, turned into the gaming of blind, objective algorithms comprising *likes* and shares, costs per click (CPC) and revenues.

Indeed, there is a growing movement to take back curation from the tyranny of algorithms. A world of postfact truthiness has made imperative a human touch from trusted sources in decision making. As such, we ask our Facebook hivemind what to see abroad and what to buy, which schools to put our kids in, and which doctors are best.

Millennials, a group with rising spending power and a penchant for time saved, are driving the curation wave. Facebook, Instagram, and Snapchat news feeds are as much fixtures of our days as e-mail. Our Netflix cue and order histories on Seamless, Blue Apron, or Instacart are the fixtures of the night (see https://www.ft.com/content/f81ac17a-68ae-11e8-b6eb-4acfcfb08c11; https://www.entrepreneur.com/article/305794; https://www.forbes.com/sites/forbescoachescouncil/2017/09/14/the-millennial-curation-wave-pushing-back-against-automation; https://www.lexingtonlaw.com/blog/credit-cards/millennial-spending-habits.html; https://www.smartinsights.com/social-media-marketing/social-media-strategy/new-global-social-media-research).

Our feeds and lists are precious real estate. And to the end of renting our attention, the Facebooks, Googles, Amazons, and Apples of the world are pouring in their billions toward ownership through vertical control and distribution. Which is to say, they've mostly become our default platforms for searching, buying, selling, delivering, and consumption, both in business and in pleasure (see https://www.nytimes.com/2017/03/21/magazine/platform-companies-are-becoming-more-powerful-but-what-exactly-do-they-want.html).

But there is hope yet for our inborn freedom of curation. The fractionation of our mainstream media has meant a bloom of independent outfits like BuzzFeed, VICE Vox, and Mic. E-mail newsletters like The Hustle, The What List, RadReads, and Wait But Why expound upon particularly interesting, popular, or clever small bouquets (or long reads) of tech news and mental floss, pop culture, science, literature, music, and whatever else comes to the authors' minds.

Thousands of podcasts cover every shade of subject matter: Death, Sex & Money, Freakonomics, History of Pirates, Zero to Scale, and Generation Z, even the Missing Richard Simmons. Well, Pod Save America.

Everything from stock photos to the travel industry is coming up with *bespoke* solutions, many of which are free or inexpensive and yet high quality. Unsplash and Death to the Stock Photo send curated and completely royalty-free photos to subscribers' inbox each week.

In the eternal hipster search for *authentic experiences*, there is a host of bespoke organizers at the ready, starting with Airbnb and a thousand alternatives. For instance, there is HikeMob, pitched as "road-tripping meets ridesharing," as well as TripAdvisor and affiliates, among many others (see https://www.livemint.com/Leisure/HzlsTOP4rA7qXHuoK-soYfK/Curated-experiences-are-the-next-big-travel-trend.html; https://www.hikemob.com).

Beyond curation by mere humans, the Brave New World of Web 3.0 already has machines that have learned our patterns of consumption better than ourselves, serving up curated content, goods, and services on demand. IoT continues to enable seamless mind accommodation (see https://medium.com/@doradoico/why-ai-is-the-future-of-on-demand-delivery-9e745fec4372; https://www.forbes.com/sites/julianmitchell/2018/09/05/how-ai-machine-learning-and-other-disruptive-trends-are-defining-the-future-of-customer-service; https://www.wired.com/brandlab/2018/05/bringing-power-ai-internet-things).

"Alexa, 3-D-print my clone right now." OK, maybe in 2040. But a billionaire can dream.

Next up: sea changes in the way we shop, manage our finances, approach our health care, and retool our education. Armed with vast databases of consumer behavior, AI will soon predict our purchases and perfect mates, health problems, best investments, optimal career trajectories, and so on. While still in high school, kids will know the courses they must take in college, the best school they can get into, the best companies to work for, and the best mentors to achieve their fullest potential.

In fact, LinkedIn is rumored to be working on an AI career coach. While automation is decimating the ranks of junior lawyers, doctors, and investment managers, the gig economy has created a de facto army of contractors (see https://engineering.linkedin.com/blog/2018/10/an-introduction-to-ai-at-linkedin;https://www.linkedin.com/pulse/your-next-career-coach-might-just-ai-nicholas-jelfs-jelf; https://www.entrepreneur.com/article/295827; http://www.bbc.com/future/story/20170522-how-automation-will-affect-you-the-experts-view;https://www.mckinsey.com/featured-insights/employment-and-growth/automation-jobs-and-the-future-of-work). It looks as if there will be only one piece of advice to give: Create the Start-up of You, right now.

And if you or your parents can't afford the start-up costs, well then, tough luck. You will be left behind or perhaps forced to make your choices on your own and bootstrap.

As of late, two moguls with much riding on the AI wave, Mark Zuckerberg and Elon Musk, have pitched a public battle of ideas regarding risks to humans from AI. Musk thinks machines will make us slaves or mincemeat, while Zuckerberg maintains it's all just helpful optimizing for the best decisions. Judge as you will: Facebook shut down its own AI in 2017 when it created a new language (see https://www.forbes.com/sites/quora/2017/08/16/why-facebook-shut-down-its-artificial-intelligence-program-that-went-rogue).

This brings us back to human nature, which remains the same. The trait that separates us from all animals remains our ability to choose, beyond the dictations of our sympathetic nervous system. Whether or not we outsource our decisions to machines, mothers will still know best (grandmothers, even better). We'll all still have the curiosity to know what happens when we go off script.

So rest assured, millennial curator, you will not be automated. Not today, at least.

***

In the age of the ubiquitous millennial, as goes Brooklyn, so goes the entire Union. One look at Williamsburg and its environs and their incredible transformation from half-industrial, half-ghetto artist haven to ultra-sleek luxury high-rises and loft buildings plus start-up offices and luxury boutiques for trust fund hipsters and Wall Street mavens, concert, and conference venues, with elegant graffiti signaling the latest in fashion and film, is nothing if not miraculous.

Now replace Brooklyn with parts of Los Angeles, Boston, Philadelphia, St. Louis, Houston, Miami, Denver, Seattle, or just about any major metro area in the United States—even Detroit—and you'll see a similar trend long unfolding. Fly into Mexico City or Tel Aviv, Paris, London, Barcelona, or a hundred other cities around the world, and you'll see much the same sort of scene unfold with equal effect.

Trendy coffee shops sit chock-full with craft coffee-swilling millennial freelancers and gigsters working on their laptops all day, across the street from outlets of major chains like Lululemon, Chipotle, Panera, and Apple. The cornerstone of the neighborhood is often a Whole Foods where hipsters spend their trust fund money—or the little they have left over after paying for rent, utilities, and Wi-Fi—on everything from quinoa to organic kumquats, artisanal seltzer to craft beer, overpriced pole-caught tuna, and frozen organic stir fry mix, plus hand-grown supplements, ethically sourced, fair trade cosmetics, and the like.

Countless downtowns, large and small, have become reinvigorated with an influx of millennials moving into seedier areas with lower rent, driving in real estate developers, who drive up real estate prices, bring in major chains, gentrify the hood, drive out the artists and diverse locals, and attract the trust fund and financier crowds, in turn driving up prices and standards for everything.

But this transformation comes at a high cost—and not just for the local, often much poorer, residents who face higher rents, overpriced groceries, and the other charming side effects of gentrification.

For millennials themselves, the cycle of ever-higher rents and an increasing cost of living despite stagnant wages, underemployment, and rather low—and shrinking—social mobility means an ever slower progression toward full employment with a livable wage in one's chosen field, paying off student loans, cohabitation, then marriage, children and large asset ownership, meaningful savings, investment, and retirement.

Back in Williamsburg, the contrast could not be starker between the northern part—that of luxury dorms for trust fund millennials, Lululemon, and craft coffee—and the south— a Satmar Chassidic neighborhood with dramatically higher unemployment, high poverty, and much less expensive housing and groceries. If not for the traditional mores and strong (and isolated, quickly growing due to high birth rate) communal presence of the

Chassidic community, it is quite certain that real estate developers would have long taken over the rest of the neighborhood and driven out the residents from rent-controlled and community-subsidized apartments.

When we look at the rest of the picture, that eternal millennial optimism about the future is in some places well justified, and in others, dimmed by stark reality. On the one hand, the growth of—and investment in—Silicon Alley (New York City's tech scene, which includes a burgeoning part in Brooklyn) and other start-up hubs in Denver, Atlanta, Austin, Los Angeles, and elsewhere has been quite remarkable. On the other hand, the FAANG cartel has stifled or acqui-hired and shut down a large number of companies over the last few years, leading to plateaued innovation by new market entrants in certain sectors of tech, due to high costs of entry. But overall, the center of gravity in tech has shifted away from Silicon Valley to New York and the other aforementioned major urban areas, drawing a large number of millennial coders, founders, operators, and funders to create a thriving start-up ecosystem with support from New York City, various foundations, and private individuals.

The artisanal food movement has also had its share of scandals, not least among them being the Mast "Artisanal," $10-a-bar chocolate fiasco. True artisans simply can't afford the sky-high rent in Williamsburg, unless they've just left finance, law, or consulting with substantial savings to spend on start-up capital and overhead, to open a bar or restaurant or a skateboard-and-flower store (albeit in another, almost as gentrified, part of Brooklyn).

And this goes double for artists and other creatives without parental or institutional support, forcing them to move further and further out from population centers, eventually driving them out of over-gentrified cities, creating a vacuum filled by chain stores and eateries favored by landlords who happily price out small businesses.

Not only has Amazon come to own Whole Foods, making a Prime membership indispensable for discounted groceries, but consolidation and corporatization have become the norm, rather than the exception.

To be sure, cities go through their own economic cycles and Brooklyn and the others are no exception. One need look no further than the quickly materializing effect of the impending L train shutdown in 2019 on Williamsburg rents coming back down to earth. But the seemingly endless supply of ambitious young college grads from upper-middle class families has long prevented any sustained drop in real estate prices—whether lease or purchase—to make housing meaningfully affordable for those not as well-heeled, highly indebted, and mostly just getting by with stagnant wages that prevent them from meaningful savings for a home or car purchase, from marrying younger (or at all).

The worrying part about this trend is that even those millennials comfortably in the 1 percent (hedge funders and other financiers, professional services workers, and selected others), making $500,000 a year in combined salary, with two kids, are still unable to save more than a few thousand dollars a year, after taxes, schooling, mortgage payments, property taxes, food, car payments, and the rather average expenses factored to New York prices.

Granted, New York may be an extreme example, along with San Francisco and D.C. suburbs, but even *affordable* cities that have seen a large influx of millennials of all ages in the last decade, such as Atlanta and Philadelphia, have seen real estate prices creep up to unsustainable levels, and with them, higher food and other prices.

It is almost certain that a real estate bubble, along with a student loan and other bubbles, will burst in 2019 or 2020, leading to a recession. While it will certainly bring real estate prices back down to earth in most overheated places, there is little insurance against a new wave of institutional and private investors snapping up distressed real estate and driving the prices right back up within 2 to 3 years, leading to price gains that far outstrip wage growth and asset depreciation during a recession.

It is also worrisome to imagine the death of yet new business models and redundant roles in the next recession, thanks to increasing automation, out- and in-sourcing, part-time/gig employment, and other forces that leave younger, less experienced workers at a disadvantage without advanced education, client experience, and immediate value to an enterprise. This is where companies will have to step up remedial education—that is, unless they can more easily have experienced labor for less elsewhere or without spending on benefits. Hence, the discussion of a universal basic income (UBI), which has gone nowhere, to date.

And so, today we have both very well-off and very resourceful millennials clinging on to their hipster lifestyle in urban areas until the next crash. Unemployment at record lows, a booming economy, but very few are actually sharing in its gains. Student loan forgiveness is but a pipe dream, even for those in public service for 10 years (standing at a measly 1 percent, due to fine print that is beyond Byzantine). The savings rate is nonexistent at 2.4 percent and getting worse for the majority of Americans of all generations.

Race relations are at a low. Gender relations are in a terrible state with the #MeToo reckoning. Political correctness is at its peak, even as liberals find it perfectly safe to bash Trump relentlessly. Partisanship in politics is seemingly beyond repair. Every day seems to bring a new regulation or policy designed to screw millennials even further, whether it's regarding student loan repayment or forgiveness, a tax overhaul back-loaded with a tax hike for the non-1 percent, an assault on entitlement programs, and so on. Everyone is bracing for a crash sooner or later.

Whether or not the next recession brings social unrest, demonstrations, a radical reaction by the administration, or otherwise a change in administrations and a fresh approach, is anyone's guess, as of this writing. But the ingredients for mass unrest are definitely in place, with the booming economy and an ultrafast news cycle, a fig leaf barely hanging on, for now.

Millennials have largely joined protests started by Gen X and Gen Z, to date, otherwise participating in *safe* political activity under the liberal umbrella. Whether—and how— millennials will assume their own mantle of political, workplace, and other leadership in times of difficulty is anyone's guess. Conflict and risk avoidance can hold as an ethos only for so long, under the circumstances.

For the time being, hipster oases in Brooklyn and elsewhere around the country are safe and sound, with craft coffee and croissants, fancy beer, Netflix, and weed keeping the millennials hopeful and at bay, if anxious behind the facade—and at a crossroads.

***

Summary

The Brooklynization of Millennials—how millennial aesthetics are influenced by both the Do-It-Yourself (DIY)/ start-up movement and Lululemon, Whole Foods, Amazon, and rising rents, democratization and yet disenfranchisement of the Creative Class all over the United States, where downtowns have turned from ghettoes to loft-filled creative havens; increasing wealth gap between the trust fund kids and young professionals and high school grads and dropouts (discussion of how upward mobility has continued to shrink and what it means for our work, life, and career)

CHAPTER 11

Conclusion: A Blueprint for Success

Throughout this book, we've covered the many ways in which millennials are, for the most part, anything but problem children or entitled, but rather just like all generations before them, in most regards, for what they want out of work and life, just delayed and impatient to catch up.

The first thing other generations must do when dealing with us is to treat us like the adults we are, listen carefully to us, learn our language and psychology, and then leverage it.

The reason it's incumbent on companies to be proactive with millennials, rather than reactive and condescending, is simple demographics, plus the stark supply–demand disparity between business needs and the millennial talent available or trainable to meet them.

Just as companies budget for any number of things each year, including certain benefits, a sales team, cost of goods sold, and recruitment costs, providing millennial employees with a superior employee experience need neither break the bank nor simply watch millennial employees leave quickly. The specifics have been laid out in detail earlier on.

To get the best out of us, employers, advisers, mentors, investors, and all other stakeholders in our businesses and lives must focus simply on helping us become the best versions of ourselves as professionals and humans, equally. While this may look and feel quite different to their own experiences as employees just keeping their head down and working hard, a failure to understand and embrace the millennial ethos at work is an expensive mistake to make, simply due to demographics and workplace demand in light of job market supply.

In short, while it requires patience and lots of listening, seemingly *coddling* millennials with relevant benefits, regular feedback and coaching, dedicated tech and L&D budget, among others, and creating an excellent EX is a benefit to *all* employees and executives, as well as the brand and the bottom line, not just individual millennials.

In light of the large and quickly growing millennial spending power, businesses catering to millennials have long learned to accommodate millennial tastes, worldviews, and shopping habits. They are now learning, often the hard way, that the best customer experience starts with a great employee experience.

As for millennials ourselves, *the kids are alright*. You know, sort of, #KiddingNotKidding. <Nervous laugh>

While most of us may be flying under the radar, putting out best face forward to the world, many of us are just doing our best to do work we love, enjoy life through experiences, not smother ourselves with anxiety over maintaining some perceived status, while plodding along in life, hedging, avoiding risk and making difficult decisions, not overly worried about buying or renting a car or house unless truly necessary. There's always room for optimism, even if we're feeling screwed already and getting more screwed by the day. Life is full of excitement and adventure, exotic food, trips to new places, plus lots of simple, pleasant things that don't require a lot of money or stuff to enjoy.

But we can clearly do better than just fly under the radar and hope for the best, while clinging to outmoded career and financial advice in a rapidly changing world. Since we can't magically fast-forward to a time when we millennials have meaningful political and corporate boardroom power, our focus should, as always, be on taking ownership of our own stories, careers, businesses, and finances, plus embracing the chip on our collective shoulder from being the most bashed generation of all time, prove boomers wrong, get our collective stuff together, and focus on changing attitudes, then policies, then rules and regulations, and ultimately laws to reverse the trend of older politicians eating our proverbial lunch, dinner, and breakfast, too.

We *are* adults and must act as such, which means taking responsibility for ourselves, our families, and each other, as well as for our present and for improving our lives for our actual or future children's future.

The life lessons I've learned in my experience as an *old* millennial—one who's changed careers four times, lived through massive challenges and setbacks, plus met tens of thousands of people and heard and processed their human stories, coached hundreds through life and career transformation—are shared next, in parting.

If you see something, say something. If you say something, make it count. Write it down and share it with others. Gather people together to demand change. Press for it long enough to get it. Start small, but don't play small ball forever.

Vote with your feet. Own your problems. Fail forward and learn quickly. Take intelligent risks. Be resourceful and learn the rules; then follow them long enough to absorb their importance before you try to break them. Get a coach or five (not a mentor) to help you thrive, not just survive. Demand something greater of yourself than complacency and hope, but don't be handcuffed by impossible expectations. Don't look left or right and focus only on your own potential and fulfilling it.

Escape the cage of your thinking and small-mindedness every single day. Rise up like a lion. Be always the head, never the tail.

Be loyal and engaged with yourself and your life mission and values. Share the wealth of your skills and experience with others. Always look to add value to others before you ask for anything. If you don't ask, the answer is always no. Always seek to be part of the solution, not the problem.

Finally, seek truth in all situations, messages, and people, not happiness or pleasure. It's much harder to find and gather, but carries the greatest rewards in life.

Do your life's best work now, not mañana, mañana [tomorrow, tomorrow]. Live your best life today, not next year. Strive to leave others better off for having met you than they were before. Think local, act global.

And don't forget to smell the roses when you're out there conquering or saving the world.

***

Summary

Conclusion: A Blueprint for Success—what millennials need to do in order to tangibly improve their lives, careers, and businesses; what employers, investors, advisers, and others need to do in order to get the best out of us, including our energy and efforts, spending power, and engagement and loyalty

THE END

Resources/Further Reading

Accenture Millennial Shopper Survey—Who Are the Millennial Shoppers? And What Do They Really Want? https://www.accenture.com/us-en/insight-outlook-who-are-millennial-shoppers-what-do-they-really-want-retail

Go Ahead, Millennials; Destroy Us, https://www.nytimes.com/2018/03/02/opinion/go-ahead-millennials-destroy-us.html

Goldman Sachs—Millennials Coming of Age, https://www.goldmansachs.com/insights/archive/millennials/

Here are 70 Things Millennials Have Killed: https://mashable.com/2017/07/31/things-millennials-have-killed/#aDdaDS03VZqw

How Millennials and Gen Zs will Transform the 2018 Workplace, https://www.inc.com/ryan-jenkins/how-millennials-and-generation-z-will-transform-2018-workplace.html

http://strategyonline.ca/2016/02/17/how-millennials-see-themselves/

https://www.benzinga.com/news/18/08/12258506/how-the-real-economy-has-fared-during-the-longest-bull-market-in-history

https://www.curbed.com/2017/12/11/16754822/millennials-2018-election-city-hall-local-races

https://www.economist.com/open-future/2018/04/20/download-and-read-our-special-report-on-how-millennials-can-help-themselves-reach-their-full-potential

https://www.inc.com/bill-green/whats-holding-back-todays-millennial-entrepreneurs-and-what-they-need-to-succeed.html

https://www.marketingcharts.com/demographics-and-audiences-58789

https://www.nggconsult.com/millennials-showdown/

https://www.ozy.com/acumen/the-truth-about-millennials-and-work-ethic/74709

https://www.qualtrics.com/millennials/

https://www.thedailybeast.com/the-screwed-millennial-generation-gets-smart

Millennials and the Labor Force (Trends in 2018), https://www
.advisorperspectives.com/dshort/updates/2018/10/10/millennials-
and-the-labor-force-a-look-at-the-trends

Office Perks: Millennial Expectations Change What Employers Offer,
https://www.reportlinker.com/insight/office-perks.html

Report: Trends in Job Tenure—and What Employers Should Do About
Them. http://blog.indeed.com/2017/06/29/trends-job-tenure/

The Biggest Stereotype about Millennials at Work is Wrong, https://
qz.com/961243/us-millennials-stay-in-their-jobs-just-as-long-as-
previous-generations/

The Deloitte Millennial Survey 2018, Millennials' confidence in business, loyalty to employers deteriorate. Respondents yearn for leaders whose decisions might benefit the world—and their careers, https://www2.deloitte
.com/global/en/pages/about-deloitte/articles/millennialsurvey.html

The Malicious Politics of Millennial Bashing, https://newrepublic.com/
article/144237/malicious-politics-millennial-bashing

This is What Millennials Want in 2018, https://www.weforum.org/
agenda/2018/01/this-is-what-millennials-want-in-2018/

Ultimate Collection of data on Millennial Engagement and Loyalty,
https://blog.accessperks.com/millennial-employee-engagement-
loyalty-statistics-the-ultimate-collection

Selected "Further Reading" references are above; the other references are
listed below:

http://apps.urban.org/features/wealth-inequality-charts/

http://customerthink.com/an-inconvenient-truth-93-of-customer-
experience-initiatives-are-failing/

http://fortune.com/2016/02/20/millennial-entrepreneurs-study/

http://library.cqpress.com/cqresearcher/document.php?id=cqresrre2017
120100

http://nymag.com/intelligencer/2018/02/florida-shooting-survivor-gets-
nra-death-threats-on-facebook.html

http://theconversation.com/millennials-are-so-over-us-domination-of-
world-affairs-99167

http://time.com/5357204/july-unemployment-rate/

http://www.latimes.com/opinion/opinion-la/la-ol-millennials-less-sex-20160802-snap-story.html

http://pewforum.org/2010/02/17/religion-among-the-millennials/

http://pewresearch.org/fact-tank/2015/11/23/millennials-are-less-religious-than-older-americans-but-just-as-spiritual/

http://pewresearch.org/fact-tank/2016/01/08/qa-why-millennials-are-less-religious-than-older-americans/

http://pewresearch.org/fact-tank/2017/04/19/millennials-arent-job-hopping-any-faster-than-generation-x-did/

http://pewresearch.org/fact-tank/2017/09/06/5-facts-about-millennial-households/

http://pewresearch.org/fact-tank/2018/03/16/how-millennials-compare-with-their-grandparents/

http://pewresearch.org/fact-tank/2018/04/09/gender-pay-gap-facts/

http://pewresearch.org/fact-tank/2018/05/02/millennials-stand-out-for-their-technology-use-but-older-generations-also-embrace-digital-life/

http://pewresearch.org/fact-tank/2018/05/02/millennials-stand-out-for-their-technology-use-but-older-generations-also-embrace-digital-life/

https://abcnews.go.com/Politics/kavanaugh-accuser-victimized-coming-forward-story/story?id=58341975

https://app.hedgeye.com/insights/68981-millennials-are-a-risk-averse-generation?type=policy

https://arstechnica.com/tech-policy/2018/01/lawsuit-goes-after-alleged-anti-conservative-bias-at-google/

https://atlanta.curbed.com/2018/4/17/17247758/atlanta-housing-prices-sales-remax

https://bigthink.com/philip-perry/millennials-are-at-higher-risk-for-mental-health-issues-this-may-be-why

https://blog.interface.com/

https://blog.nada.org/2018/04/09/the-future-of-personal-vehicle-ownership/

https://campuspress.yale.edu/perspective/are-millennials-healthier-than-the-baby-boomers/

https://en.wikipedia.org/wiki/Acqui-hiring

https://en.wikipedia.org/wiki/One-dollar_salary

https://en.wikipedia.org/wiki/Strauss-Howe_generational_theory

https://en.wikipedia.org/wiki/Xennials

https://enjoy.thegreatecourseadventure.com/why-are-97-of-people-failing/

https://family.findlaw.com/marriage/same-sex-marriage-and-federal-benefits.html

https://gizmodo.com/google-removes-nearly-all-mentions-of-dont-be-evil-from-1826153393

https://hbr.org/2016/08/millennials-are-actually-workaholics-according-to-research

https://hbr.org/2016/08/millennials-are-actually-workaholics-according-to-research

https://hbr.org/2016/08/millennials-are-actually-workaholics-according-to-research

https://highline.huffingtonpost.com/articles/en/poor-millennials/

https://impact.vice.com/en_us/article/gy57km/millennials-are-engaging-in-political-action-now-more-than-ever

https://inequality.org/great-divide/how-to-track-ceo-worker-pay-ratios/

https://learning.linkedin.com/resources/workplace-learning-report-2018

https://medium.com/neodotlife/millennials-and-drugs-23aa24b8fb1d

https://medium.com/the-mission/the-14-most-destructive-millennial-myths-debunked-by-data-aa00838eecd6

https://money.usnews.com/money/retirement/articles/2014/07/28/workplace-benefits-that-are-disappearing

https://nypost.com/2016/07/04/im-a-millennial-and-my-generation-sucks/

https://nypost.com/2018/02/16/millennials-are-an-amazingly-patient-bunch/

https://obamawhitehouse.archives.gov/sites/default/files/docs/millennials_report.pdf

https://people.com/celebrity/employees-who-were-fired-because-of-social-media-posts/

https://philly.curbed.com/2017/4/7/15209526/philadelphia-housing-rental-statistics-pew-report

https://priceonomics.com/which-generation-is-most-distracted-by-their/

https://qz.com/571151/the-mast-brothers-fooled-the-world-into-buying-crappy-hipster-chocolate-for-10-a-bar/

https://russiapedia.rt.com/on-this-day/july-17/

https://seekingalpha.com/article/4184389-howe-risk-averse-millennials-blamed-startups-decline

https://talentorganizationblog.accenture.com/financialservices/making-the-connection-between-cx-and-ex-a-recipe-for-competitive-advantage

https://technical.ly/brooklyn/2018/07/31/alice-fintech-startup-payroll-benefits/?utm_campaign=Brooklyn%20Editorial%20Email&utm_source=hs_email&utm_medium=email&utm_content=65579021&_hsenc=p2ANqtz--7v-P-qo2dzxcWcnmZ8G8R6w9r4F-Hno-uSwiR4OXQpIgdJYn-aF4Udvgoh2Wxce7gPBgzDstW0zX17aoQKePylNDv7AA&_hsmi=65579021

https://thenextweb.com/hardfork/2018/09/18/cryptocurrency-bitcoin-blockchain-wallet/

https://tradingeconomics.com/united-states/unemployment-rate

https://trend.pewtrusts.org/en/archive/winter-2018/the-millennials-arent-kids-anymore

https://www.aarp.org/work/small-business/info-2018/self-employed-numbers-fd.html

https://www.alistdaily.com/strategy/different-generations-play-video-games-platforms-genres/

https://www.bbc.com/news/world-us-canada-33290341

https://www.benefitspro.com/2016/08/15/how-much-has-same-sex-marriage-changed-employee-be/?slreturn=20181014074127

https://www.bloomberg.com/graphics/2016-millennial-generation-in-congress/

https://www.bloombergquint.com/pursuits/millennials-are-causing-the-u-s-divorce-rate-to-plummet#gs.8=HYTpI

https://www.brookings.edu/blog/social-mobility-memos/2018/01/11/raj-chetty-in-14-charts-big-findings-on-opportunity-and-mobility-we-should-know/

https://www.brookings.edu/wp-content/uploads/2018/01/2018-jan_brookings-metro_millennials-a-demographic-bridge-to-americas-diverse-future.pdf

https://www.businessinsider.com/bowel-cancer-is-on-the-rise-among-
millennials-2018-6?IR=T

https://www.businessinsider.in/Millennials-are-dragging-down-beer-
sales-but-Gen-Z-marks-a-turning-point-that-will-cause-an-even-
bigger-problem-for-the-industry/articleshow/63017397.cms

https://www.businessinsider.in/Millennials-eating-habits-are-wildly-
different-from-their-parents-and-the-food-industry-has-to-face-
urgent-consequences/articleshow/63162522.cms

https://www.businessinsider.in/One-largely-overlooked-trend-in-US-
inequality-could-be-the-most-alarming/articleshow/59638553.cms

https://www.bustle.com/p/millennials-are-the-most-romantic-genera-
tion-survey-finds-8211095

https://www.cdc.gov/media/releases/2018/p0329-drug-overdose-deaths
.html

https://www.census.gov/content/dam/Census/library/working-
papers/2018/demo/SEHSD-WP-2018-09.pdf

https://www.cfr.org/report/case-wage-insurance

https://www.chicagotribune.com/business/success/inc/tca-the-open-
office-plan-is-backfiring-20180220-story.html

https://www.clomedia.com/2017/09/11/job-hoppers/

https://www.cnbc.com/2015/06/08/deutsche-bank-why-the-dual-ceo-
system-failed.html

https://www.cnbc.com/2017/03/24/budget-breakdown-of-couple-
making-500000-a-year-and-feeling-average.html

https://www.cnbc.com/2017/09/14/millennials-are-more-financially-
responsible-than-boomers-or-gen-x.html

https://www.cnbc.com/2018/04/11/generation-x--not-millennials--is-
changing-the-nature-of-work.html

https://www.cnbc.com/2018/04/11/generation-x--not-millennials--is-
changing-the-nature-of-work.html

https://www.cnbc.com/2018/06/06/us-house-prices-are-going-to-rise-
at-twice-the-speed-of-inflation-and-pay-reuters-poll.html

https://www.cnbc.com/2018/08/24/the-longest-bull-then-and-now-
how-financial-conditions-have-changed.html

https://www.cnbc.com/2018/09/18/larry-kudlows-entitlement-reform-
talk-sparks-democratic-attacks.html

https://www.cnbc.com/2018/09/21/the-education-department-data-shows-how-rare-loan-forgiveness-is.html

https://www.economist.com/united-states/2018/09/27/anti-discrimination-statements-by-employers

https://www.entrepreneur.com/article/306687

https://www.epi.org/nominal-wage-tracker/

https://www.fastcompany.com/40497318/how-millennials-are-trying-to-revive-the-labor-movement

https://www.forbes.com/sites/forbescoachescouncil/2016/12/01/how-to-attract-and-retain-millennials-and-get-them-to-do-their-lifes-best-work-for-you/#2e4583ee4e70

https://www.forbes.com/sites/forbescoachescouncil/2017/08/08/the-importance-of-customer-experience-in-the-age-of-instant-gratification/#32120a6b60e1

https://www.forbes.com/sites/forbescoachescouncil/2017/09/14/the-millennial-curation-wave-pushing-back-against-automation/#2060be1a8b03

https://www.forbes.com/sites/kimjay/2017/08/25/warning-its-easier-now-than-ever-before-to-become-an-entrepreneur/#3333a709505f

https://www.forbes.com/sites/larryalton/2017/02/15/are-millennials-more-or-less-likely-to-start-their-own-businesses/#74939a2b1301

https://www.forbes.com/sites/micahsolomon/2018/05/03/for-small-business-week-all-about-millennial-consumers-and-millennial-friendly-customer-experiences/#2d3d0b6b2f91

https://www.forbes.com/sites/petergeorgescu/2018/08/22/americas-real-economy-it-isnt-booming/#2dd6da2160b7

https://www.forbes.com/sites/spencerbogart/2017/11/08/7-stats-that-highlight-a-millennial-propensity-for-bitcoin/#632988e532c4

https://www.forbes.com/sites/zackfriedman/2018/06/13/student-loan-debt-statistics-2018/#6f7e0fd77310

https://www.ft.com/content/81343d9e-187b-11e8-9e9c-25c814761640

https://www.ft.com/content/e1f5416e-4eb8-11e8-ac41-759eee1efb74

https://www.healthaffairs.org/doi/abs/10.1377/hlthaff.2010.0806

https://www.inc.com/anne-gherini/gen-z-is-about-to-outnumber-millennials-heres-how-that-will-affect-business-world.html

https://www.inc.com/magazine/201511/paul-keegan/does-more-pay-mean-more-growth.html

https://www.inc.com/magazine/201511/paul-keegan/does-more-pay-mean-more-growth.html

https://www.inc.com/melanie-curtin/millennials-are-flocking-to-this-new-kind-of-communal-housing.html

https://www.investopedia.com/articles/investing/070815/are-millennials-risk-averse-or-risk-takers.asp

https://www.investopedia.com/terms/f/faang-stocks.asp

https://www.lakeviewhealth.com/resources/addiction/crisis-millennials/

https://www.laweekly.com/news/millennials-marijuana-usage-has-risen-but-pales-to-baby-boomers-hazy-days-7386719

https://www.marketwatch.com/story/here-are-all-of-the-things-millennials-have-been-accused-of-killing-2017-05-22

https://www.mckinsey.com/industries/capital-projects-and-infrastruc-ture/our-insights/meeting-millennials-where-they-shop-shaping-the-future-of-shopping-malls

https://www.npr.org/2017/07/05/535626109/the-end-of-loyalty-and-the-decline-of-good-jobs-in-america

https://www.npr.org/2018/07/29/633686806/the-myth-of-the-self-made-millennial

https://www.nytimes.com/2017/01/27/technology/millennial-social-media-usage.html

https://www.nytimes.com/2018/05/29/well/mind/millennials-love-marriage-sex-relationships-dating.html

https://www.nytimes.com/2018/05/29/well/mind/millennials-love-marriage-sex-relationships-dating.html

https://www.nytimes.com/2018/06/27/nyregion/alexandria-ocasio-cortez.html

https://www.nytimes.com/2018/09/26/sports/nike-colin-kaepernick.html

https://www.ontheclock.com/Blog/employee-engagement-statistics.aspx

https://www.phillyvoice.com/will-millennials-ever-go-meme-wewe/

https://www.psychologytoday.com/us/blog/our-changing-culture/201602/do-millennials-have-lesser-work-ethic

https://www.researchgate.net/publication/309006000_Generational_
Differences_in_Work_Ethic_Fact_or_Fiction

https://www.restaurant-hospitality.com/food-trends/sriracha-ranks-
go-condiment-millennials

https://www.reuters.com/article/us-usa-election-millennials/
exclusive-democrats-lose-ground-with-millennials-reuters-ipsos-poll-
idUSKBN1I10YH

https://www.rollcall.com/news/politics/millennials-shake-congress-
next-session

https://www.salon.com/2018/03/25/how-you-got-screwed-by-the-
education-system/

https://www.sbfi.com/design-news-insight/workplace-design-trends-
2018/

https://www.sfgate.com/burningman/article/Burning-Man-sober-
Anonymous-Village-camp-no-drugs-13169304.php

https://www.statista.com/statistics/246234/personal-savings-rate-
in-the-united-states/

https://www.strategy-business.com/article/00318?gko=c7329

https://www.td.org/insights/millennials-the-risk-averse-generation

https://www.theamericanconservative.com/dreher/smartphones-
are-our-soma/

https://www.theatlantic.com/business/archive/2016/01/zappos-
holacracy-hierarchy/424173/

https://www.theatlantic.com/business/archive/2016/01/zappos-
holacracy-hierarchy/424173/

https://www.theatlantic.com/business/archive/2016/07/why-are-so-
many-millennials-having-children-out-of-wedlock/491753/

https://www.transamericacenter.org/docs/default-source/retirement-survey-
of-workers/tcrs2018_sr_18th_annual_worker_compendium.pdf?utm_
source=Sailthru&utm_medium=email&utm_campaign=Millennials%20
High%20on%20Life%20Insurance%20NewsWire2018-
07-17T14:19:39%2B00:00jwm&utm_term=Millennials%20
High%20on%20Life%20Insurance%20NewsWire2018-07-17
T14:19:39%2B00:00jwm

https://www.trulia.com/research/homeownership-q118/

https://www.usatoday.com/story/money/2016/04/23/pensions-economy-workers/83292892/

https://www.vox.com/2018/6/27/17509858/alexandria-ocasio-cortez-women-media

https://www.vox.com/the-big-idea/2018/7/11/17559484/gig-economy-jobs-rooted-rootless-moving-job-hopping-millennials

https://www.washingtonpost.com/news/fact-checker/wp/2018/01/12/is-the-trump-tax-cut-good-or-bad-for-the-middle-class/?noredirect=on&utm_term=.a5407fb4e647

https://www.washingtonpost.com/news/in-theory/wp/2016/03/24/millennials-are-significantly-more-progressive-than-their-parents/?noredirect=on&utm_term=.7f9142b491a3

https://www.washingtonpost.com/news/to-your-health/wp/2018/05/10/why-kids-and-teens-may-face-far-more-anxiety-these-days/

https://www.washingtonpost.com/news/wonk/wp/2016/09/07/young-people-are-committing-much-less-crime-older-people-are-still-behaving-as-badly-as-before/?utm_term=.d484e6498202

https://www.weforum.org/agenda/2018/04/the-worlds-biggest-economies-in-2018/

https://www.wework.com/creator/how-to-guides/employee-child-care-benefits/

https://www.ypulse.com/post/view/5-stats-that-prove-gen-z-millennials-only-eat-healthy-ish

https://www2.deloitte.com/insights/us/en/focus/human-capital-trends/2018/employee-well-being-programs.html

About the Author

Yuri Kruman is a corporate HR transformation /employee experience (EX) consultant, board member, startup advisor, official member of the Forbes Coaches Council, and contributor to Forbes, Entrepreneur, Business.com, Influencive, and others. Yuri's consulting, advising, and coaching portfolio includes speaking engagements, workshops, and advisory work on personal plus professional development focused on employee experience (EX), HR transformation/change management, customer experience (CX), PR/media and business strategy, impacting thousands of Fortune 500 and startup executives. He is the author of the forthcoming book *Mastering The Talk to Master Your Life* (2019).

A regular guest on top podcasts such as *Entrepreneur on Fire, Wharton Business Radio, As Told By Nomads and Conscious Millionaire,* he's also been published or featured on *Inc., Fast Co., Time, Mashable, PBS and BBC.* Yuri trains client teams on ways to maximize their EX, especially talent retention, learning and development using storytelling, and branding and proprietary personal development strategies.

Index

OTHER TITLES IN THE HUMAN RESOURCE MANAGEMENT AND ORGANIZATIONAL BEHAVIOR COLLECTION

- *The HOW of Leadership: Inspire People to Achieve Extraordinary Results* by Maxwell Ubah
- *Lead Self First Before Leading Others: A Life Planning Resource* by Stephen K. Hacker and Marvin Washington
- *The Concise Coaching Handbook: How to Coach Yourself and Others to Get Business Results* by Elizabeth Dickinson
- *Leading the High-Performing Company: A Transformational Guide to Growing Your Business and Outperforming Your Competition* by Heidi Pozzo
- *How Successful Engineers Become Great Business Leaders* by Paul Rulkens
- *Creating a Successful Consulting Practice* by Gary W. Randazzo
- *Skilling India: Challenges and Opportunities* by S. Nayana Tara
- *Redefining Competency Based Education: Competence for Life* by Nina Morel
- *No Dumbing Down: A No-Nonsense Guide for CEOs on Organization Growth* by Karen D. Walker
- *From Behind the Desk to the Front of the Stage: How to Enhance Your Presentation Skills* by David Worsfold
- *The New World of Human Resources and Employment: How Artificial Intelligence and Process Redesign is Driving Dramatic Change* by Tony Miller
- *Virtual Vic: A Management Fable* by Laurence M. Rose
- *Our Glassrooms: Perceptiveness and Its Implications for Transformational Leadership* by Dhruva Trivedy
- *Leadership Insights: 11 Typical Mistakes Young Leaders Make and Tips to Avoid Them* by Matt L. Beadle
- *Temperatism, Volume II: Doing Good Through Business With a Social Conscience* by Carrie Foster
- *The Generation Myth: How to Improve Intergenerational Relationships in the Workplace* by Michael J. Urick

Announcing the Business Expert Press Digital Library

Concise e-books business students need for classroom and research

This book can also be purchased in an e-book collection by your library as

- *a one-time purchase,*
- *that is owned forever,*
- *allows for simultaneous readers,*
- *has no restrictions on printing, and*
- *can be downloaded as PDFs from within the library community.*

Our digital library collections are a great solution to beat the rising cost of textbooks. E-books can be loaded into their course management systems or onto students' e-book readers.
The **Business Expert Press** digital libraries are very affordable, with no obligation to buy in future years. For more information, please visit **www.businessexpertpress.com/librarians**.
To set up a trial in the United States, please email **sales@businessexpertpress.com**.

www.ingramcontent.com/pod-product-compliance
Lightning Source LLC
Chambersburg PA
CBHW061324220326
41599CB00026B/5018